Dear Anna

with best wishes

Sid

29.9.97.

IS MY VALLEY STILL GREEN?

Sid Peatling

MINERVA PRESS
LONDON
MONTREUX LOS ANGELES SYDNEY

IS MY VALLEY STILL GREEN?

ISBN 1 86106 601 5

First Published 1997 by
MINERVA PRESS
195 Knightsbridge
London SW7 1RE

Printed in Great Britain for Minerva Press

IS MY VALLEY STILL GREEN?

All characters and events in this book are fictional and any resemblance to actual places, events or persons, living or dead, is purely coincidental.

Acknowledgements

I have received a great deal of assistance in writing this, my first novel, too many to mention really but I must single out 'Valley Forests Initiative' of the Welsh Development agency for their help, along with Lord Archer of Weston-super-Mare for his early advice. My research led me to discover Guido Sidoli, living in retirement here in Weston-super-Mare, a source of much information for my fictional third chapter. Finally, to my wife and family for their help and encouragement as I "bounced" ideas off them.

About the Author

Sid Peatling was born in London on August 11, 1929. He was educated at Tottenham County School in London and then Tonypandy Secondary School when he moved to South Wales as an evacuee.

He is a marketing manager and his hobbies include Scouting, travel and geography.

He is currently the Scout District Press and Public Relations Officer in Weston-super-Mare.

He married Marjorie in 1950 and they have a son and a daughter.

Contents

Chapter One
Sid

This is my story!

It was scary walking home from Cub Scout meetings in January, 1940. The anti-aircraft guns in Finsbury Park, North London, were blazing away at German bombers droning away overhead, looking for a light, a railway line or a river that would indicate where they should unload their lethal cargo of bombs. Thank God for the air-raid wardens, whose cry of "Put that light out" was to become a comic catchphrase in happier, safer peacetime. The detonating ack-ack shells sprayed hot, jagged lumps of shrapnel on to the roofs of our houses, where it clattered down into the streets, as we ran home, dodging into shop doorways and air-raid shelters that offered momentary protection *en route*. Scary, yes, but exciting to a ten year old, whose Dad would have got home from work, had his tea, and already be fire-watching on top of the roof of the local "Ever Ready" factory. Fire watchers were surely some of the unsung heroes of World War Two?

"Mum, at school today, they gave us this sheet of paper about taking all of us children away from London for safety," I said with a schoolboy whine, that indicated that I did not want to leave my Mum, Dad, brothers and sister. Until my pal, Ted, who was in the Scouts with me said that he was going with his brothers, Ken and Len, and, perhaps, it would be "a bit of fun?"

Labels, gas masks and a bundle of spare clothes were all we could take on the big, double-decker, red London bus, which took us to Paddington station. "Where are we going?" I asked our teacher, Mr Baron, who was coming with us. He shrugged his shoulders and it was not until Ted's brother, Ken, who was good at reading, had a good look around and whispered, "I think we are going to Wales!" Horror and disbelief was registered all round at this news for all that we knew of Wales was what we had seen on the screen at the Saturday morning "pictures", a new film called *How Green Was My Valley*. Wales, to us kids, was a country where black-faced men, with lights on their hats, came home from work, singing at the tops of their voices. What a funny lot! And we were heading towards living there? "I would rather have the bombs," Ted said, with tears in his eyes.

Soon the motion of the train lulled tired children to sleep. "This is fun, Ted," I said, as we passed rapidly through the countryside. The train's whistle sounded and we entered a long, black tunnel and the smell of smoke from the engine filled our carriage. A sandwich and a small bottle of milk was brought round by some of the bigger kids, who spread the word that we were now in Wales, having gone under the sea through that long tunnel! They said that we would be stopping in about an hour. We had all accepted our fate by now and were actually enjoying the adventure. Rolling, green mountains were on both sides of the train, as we looked anxiously through the windows. "Look, there are some sheep." Then, "Look at that dirty, black river", were the cries, as we each kept a lookout for those men with black faces and lights on their hats! A long blast on the whistle heralded the train's arrival at a station with "Porth" on the sign. Lots of people clapped their hands, happy to see us as we got off the train. We were amazed to be directed onto another big, red, double-decker bus! This one had "Rhondda Transport" on its side rather than the "London Transport" of the start of our journey.

Mr Baron walked through the bus, reassuring us that we would soon be taken to our foster homes by local mothers and fathers, who would take great care of us. He gave us cards to write home, telling our parents that we had arrived safely and our new addresses. "That was not too bad, was it?" said Ted, whose face was smeared with the grime of engine smoke and streaked where a tear had escaped from his eyes.

We unloaded at a big school, set high on one side of a hill in a valley. Local children were waving and calling out "welcome", as we filed into the school hall, where there were chairs for us to sit facing a stage where several adults with books were sitting at tables. They spoke to us and then to a lot of adults who waited to take us home with them. "Keep in touch, Ted," I said, as my pal went off with a little, grey-haired lady in a pinafore. He waved a sad hand.

Smoothly our train-load of little Londoners emptied the hall and I was getting worried until the nice lady, the "billeting officer" smiled down at me and said, "Sidney, as you are the only one left, you had better come home with me."

How could a Cockney ten year old know that a lifetime of romance and adventure was opened up with that short statement? "Call me Ma," said the nice lady, as she took my hand and led me out into the sunshine. The Valley looked very green, as we walked up the hillside to number thirteen of a row of miners' cottages. "Here we are Sid. I will get Pop to make us a nice pot of tea to go with the faggots that I bought from Dick Smith's farm earlier today." That sounded good, as I had not had a proper meal since leaving home and I was hungry and more than a little anxious by now. Pop was a nice, old man, who told me stories of fighting in the trenches in World War One, where he had suffered from inhaling mustard gas as well as having a bullet go through his right hand! I knew straightaway that Pop Warner and I would get on well. He had a dog called "Laddie" and a shed full of canaries in the back garden. We listened to the wireless, every night after tea, to hear what was happening in the war and, more importantly, if there had been any more air raids on London. Sometimes we would even listen to a "Lord Haw-Haw" who, Pop said, was a traitor, as he was an Englishman on the side of the enemy. How exciting! Pop was also in the "Home Guard" and showed me the medals which he had won in the Great War.

We went out in the street to play, after school every day. The Welsh lads were great. They knew about sliding down the old coal tip on sleighs made from corrugated iron sheets, that would mysteriously appear after a walk up to the "allotments", where men grew rhubarb and vegetables to eke out our rations. The girls, who played with "whips and tops", were a good laugh, too, and we would walk in a gang up the mountain to pick windberries from little plants that grew very close to the ground. Ma Warner would then turn these into delicious pies! Yes, I was enjoying being in Wales, and so was Ted, except that we were missing our Scouts! Soon we found out that there had been a Scout troop meeting in a disused colliery building at Ynyshir, about half an hour's walk away. Getting there one evening, we were told that the leaders had been called up into the army, so Ted and I ran some games and did some knotting with the lads who had turned up. Then we found another interest for, at number six,

Miners' Cottages were Marjorie and Rita, two sisters from our "gang" and we started to go out together.

Saturday mornings were great fun, as I would go with the lads, taking a sack up the mountain to where the coal tip would heap "drams" of colliery waste, which included not only nuggets of shiny coal but, often, great lumps of wood cut from pit props! These we would carry back down the mountain to keep the fires going for the week. Saturday night was bath night – just as well! The galvanised bath came down from a hook out in the backyard and brought to the front of the kitchen fire, where black kettles of water steamed away. Pop went in first, then me! What would Mum have thought?

Everything was going well at school, too, now that I had got used to the accent. They played football with an oval ball, but I soon got used to this game called rugby and, anyway, we had proper football at Saint Luke's youth club at weekends. Oh dear, Saint David's Day was coming up and we had to learn songs in Welsh for the "eisteddfod", whatever that was. In the end it was good fun and I sang two songs in Welsh, on March 1st 1941, which was something to write home to Mum about at least.

The bombing was not quite so bad now and Mr Churchill had said on the wireless that our *Spitfires* were doing a marvellous job scaring the German bombers away! My oldest brother was in the Tank Corps and as a signaller, found the Morse code, that he had learned in the Scouts, very useful. My youngest brother and sister had been evacuated to Cheshire, so all of our family were split up now, except for mum and dad. It was about now that I wondered what boys like me, in the "Axis" enemy countries, were doing, as we heard of some of our friends' dads and brothers being killed fighting their dads and brothers in Germany, Italy and Japan.

We knew about our American allies because they were camped right here in the valley with us, and a good bunch of chaps they were, too, giving us sweets and chewing gum! My mum wrote to Ma Warner asking if she could come down to see me for a break one time. It was great to be able to show her all the adventurous things we got up to, and to take her picking blackberries, which were free! You didn't get them free in London! Mum loved it with the friendly people of the valley and said that, as the bombing was easier now, I could come home if I liked. So, I went home with Mum on the train to dirty London, and, as I had missed the eleven-plus examination, Mr

Baron arranged for me to go to Tottenham County School, (Latin motto "Nil sine Labore" which translated to "Naught without labour"), which was good, as my old Scout friends, Ben, Monty and Ron were going there, too. I was lucky again, as they played rugby at Tottenham and I had become quite good as scrum half through playing in the Rhondda Valley. Not only that, but I could get on with my First Class Scout badge! Scouting filled the adventurous need I had discovered while in the Valleys, and I was getting on well toward becoming a King's Scout, when the doodlebugs started to drop out of the sky, unannounced, save for a throbbing that suddenly stopped! No sooner had we become used to diving under our desks at school when we heard a "buzzbomb" coming, than the new "V2s" started to fall, demolishing whole streets of houses! It was time to return to Wales. A letter to Ma Warner brought an instant invitation to come back, and to bring my new baby brother with us, to live next door at number twelve. What wonderful hospitality we received from those lovely Welsh Valley folk. Calling at number six, I was told that Marjorie had diphtheria and was in the isolation hospital! Rita and I visited her there, on my first Sunday back in the Rhondda. Now that I was a grammar schoolboy, I had to travel up the Valley to Tonypandy Secondary School, (Welsh motto "Goreu Arf, Arf Dysg" which translates to "The best weapon is the weapon of learning"). The bus journey took up much of my teenage courting time although it was time to concentrate on examinations anyway. Anxious to complete my King's Scout qualification, I found that the troop was still in existence in Ynyshir, which gave me another outlet and I was awarded the badge by the District Commissioner, in August 1944. The war news on the wireless was good, until my older brother, now a paratrooper, was posted missing after the Battle of Arnhem. Now Marjorie taught me to dance, and every Saturday evening we would go to the "Rink" ballroom, in Porth, the walk home arm in arm being as enjoyable as the ballroom proximity! My final year in the green, green Rhondda Valley was one of great happiness and activity with rugby, soccer and dancing on Saturdays and going twice a week to the back row in the cinema, finishing the evening at one of the Italian-run "Bracchi" cafés with a cup of tea and a rock cake! How did I ever find the time to study for and pass the Examination of the Central Welsh Board (C.W.B) just as the war ended? I returned to London to find work as an accounts clerk, cycling to and from the West End every day to save the tube fare so that my wages could stretch to a £1. 13s. 3d. return ticket to Marjorie in Porth, once a month! Dear Ma Warner welcomed me as a son on every occasion. National service loomed! As one had to know about knotting in the Royal Navy, that was the service I asked to join for my mandatory two years. But I had tied more knots in two weeks at a Scout camp than I ever did in the Navy! Marjorie and I wrote to each other every day for those two years, were engaged at nineteen and married after demobilisation at twenty. A career in sales appealed, insurance brought in enough to get a deposit and mortgage for our first house in 1953, a memorable year, when our first child, Angela, was born, Everest was conquered, Queen Elizabeth II crowned and we bought our first car, a black Ford "Popular" for £495! Not having had the "benefit" of a public school education and being too short in stature to have been in the Guards, I found that the prospects of improving my position on the sales force of a major, evaporated milk Company were inhibited, in spite of the successes I was able to gain in merchandising and marketing the product.

Petrol rationing, resulting from the Suez Crisis, was the final straw. Our second child, David, had arrived and, as we felt there was little prospect of prospering in an England still suffering post war blues, emigration to Canada appealed. The gamble paid off when, in Toronto, the importer of a well-known range of Scottish-made marmalades and jams accepted my application to market their products on the west side of Toronto.

Eleven months later, the Marketing Director called me into his office, asking if I would take on the provinces of Manitoba and Saskatchewan for the company, arranging storage depots and hiring and training a sales force? What an opportunity! So we loaded up the car and drove to Winnipeg, Manitoba via Detroit and Chicago, tracing the source of the Mississippi en route to the Red River Valley of the popular song.

We rented a furnished house in the Fort Garry suburb of Winnipeg. Our neighbours immediately invited us in for a meal and we formed a lifelong friendship. Children went to school, Marjorie joined the local Badminton club and family life was good.

The work was hard, the distances were vast but the French Canadian, Aime Chapdelaine, who was the first salesman I hired, became a strong right arm for me and we soon started to introduce the products into the supermarkets using my one quarter million dollar marketing budget cost-effectively. In fact, Marjorie became a demonstrator of the products, spending weekends in the supermarkets offering samples of Scottish Marmalades to shoppers, a tartan sash and her Welsh accent completing the picture!

Two years later, we were on a camping vacation, when, as we were driving in the Canadian Rockies, the Royal Canadian Mounted Police flagged me down! When I confirmed my name through a nervously opened window, the Mountie said he had a message for me to phone the boss at Head Office, in Toronto, 3,000 miles away!

"What could it be? Trouble with the family in London perhaps?" An anxious phone call brought the question "Will you take over the provinces of Alberta and British Columbia? Give me a report when you get back from Alberta." What a great boss, but now I needed more help and hired Robin and Dan, in Edmonton, Alberta, to look after the northern extremities of that vast province, stretching into the romantic "Peace River Country" of the North West Territories with overtones of Nelson Eddie and Janet MacDonald, the movie stars of my childhood. I found that I could cover Calgary, where we bought a house, and most of British Columbia's potential by a monthly flight to Vancouver. As I have said, it is a big Country!

"All good things must come to an end," was an old adage come true when, in 1960, the Nestlé Company bought the company and, as they had a full sales force, it soon became apparent that there would be redundancies! Time for another gamble perhaps? "Why don't we go back to England to capitalise on this North American experience and show off our kids to their grandparents?" My childhood sweetheart agreed and it worked, when I gained the London Sales Manager's job with a progressive cigarette manufacturer. We bought a house in Hertfordshire, where we introduced our kids to Scouting and Guiding, Marjorie taking a warrant too. The village Scout Group took up much of our leisure time, until the grocery shop became available and it appealed to put some of our supermarket marketing experience to work on our own account this time.

Tesco, Sainsbury, Victor Value and Lipton all opened supermarkets during our five years in the shop, where we had created an excellent business specialising in freshly cut bacon and home-cooked hams, skills we learned as time went along.

"Distant fields are greener" as the saying goes. Angela was in Teacher Training College in Bristol. So, having spent so many nights in hotels across Canada in the previous decade, the hotel trade appealed to us and we set about finding an hotel that was both affordable and viable in the West Country, where we had taken our Scouts camping, climbing and potholing. We found what we were looking for in the fifteen-bedroomed Bay View Hotel, which proved to be a good training ground. David, now sixteen worked alongside us, as did Angela, when she could get away from college. "A rest from Scouting" was the theory, but, the evening after we had applied for the licence for our bar, a twinkle-eyed magistrate on the bench called at the hotel, announcing that he was the local District Commissioner for Scouts who had inspected our Scout camp the previous year. Our secret was out! Then the owner of the hotel next door announced that he was selling up to go into the developing nursing-home business. We made him an offer and spent all of our first winter, when we should have been resting, joining the two hotels into one thirty-two bedroomed business, having recognised that "the money was in the bedrooms"!

Angela married Alan, a nice young man whom she had met in college and who had gone to work for a bank. Business was good, the work was hard and there was a trend toward self-catering. "If we could buy a redundant farm with outbuildings that we could convert into holiday cottages," was a scheme that I put to the family one winter, meeting with tacit approval!

Doubleton Farm, a seventeenth-century farmhouse, with a traditional range of barns and stables on four acres came on the market, going to auction in the spring of 1978. We viewed, calculated, planned and took the gamble, having asked Angela and Alan to run the hotel, while we got on with the conversions. "Doubleton Farm Holiday Cottages" was up and running well by 1995, the Rhondda Borough Council's Centenary, when, as part of the celebrations, they staged an "Evacuee Reunion", which we attended, of course, joining Rita and her husband. Nostalgia came over us in waves as we were reunited with long-lost friends and sounds, sights and smells gave us much to reminisce and think about. "There is no place like home" and we had travelled more than most I suppose. Reading of a "New town" that was being built, high on the mountainside, with a mix of community and private homes, I floated the idea, "What about coming back to live in the Valleys?", knowing that I had a good business idea in the back of my mind anyway!

We considered this at length and always returned to the same question:- "IS MY VALLEY STILL GREEN?"

Chapter Two

Hans

Life was happy for Hans in his home village of Spree, which took its name from the heavily wooded peninsula in the River Spree, just ten miles south-east of Berlin. His father, Otto Ludmeyer, the warden of the forests that cradled the village and the riverbanks, had promised that they could build a tree-house for Hans' ninth birthday and Gerda, his mother, was planning a party in it when completed. "You can start writing the invitations to your friends now," Gerda called to Hans who was preparing to swim in the river.

A wet and shiny Hans emerged two hours later to ask Gerda if they could invite his cousins, Ernst, Jan and Heidi, who lived in Berlin. "They would have to come by bus and then could stay overnight, couldn't they?" Hans said, with that little boy, pleading tone in his voice. His mother agreed on the strict understanding that Hans completed all of the chores she set him to do.

Yes, life was good indeed in that summer of 1939. The grown-ups were all pleased that Herr Hitler, the Chancellor of the Third Reich for five years, was now firmly in control, after all the difficulties of the last decade. Hans was a member of the Spree Hitlerjugend Group and was hoping that he would receive a uniform as a birthday present. The older boys loved showing off their uniforms, which they had only recently been authorised to wear.

The boys paraded every week with home-made guns, as there was much talk of war and the Hitlerjugend had to be ready! It had started in Poland already and, then, England, the old enemy they had learned about in school, declared war on Germany and food and fuel became very scarce.

"At least we will not be cold this winter," Otto called to his wife, as he arrived home from work laden with bundles of wood he had trimmed, as part of his care for the forests. "Hans, you can help your father trim those boughs and cut and split some logs," Gerda called to her son, as he sat chewing his pencil writing invitations to the party. Hans loved working with his father, as he enjoyed anything to do with the forests that gave the family its living.

"I am just taking this invitation over to Gretta and will work on the firewood when I get back." Gretta was the same age as Hans and the only daughter of Mr and Mrs Rosenbaum, who lived over the tailor's shop opposite the Ludmeyer's small house. Gretta was pleased to see Hans, as she felt for him and his parents like a sister and daughter respectively, as the Rosenbaums never went cold in the winter either and her father ensured that Otto Ludmeyer was kept well supplied with working trousers in return, for such was the community spirit in this small, rural village.

The news on the wireless was good! The victorious German army had conquered Poland, then France, Holland, Belgium and Denmark. Herr Goering's *Luftwaffe* was already bombing England and it seemed that nothing could stop the Third Reich's conquest of all of Europe!

Hans and the Spree Hitlerjugend Group were bursting with pride, as they did all they could to help the war effort. Sadly, their beloved forests had to be drastically cut, to provide materials for transport-waggons as well as for fuel, and not a scrap was wasted.

At night, bombs could be heard falling and, occasionally, after an aerial battle, an enemy plane would crash on the wooded hillsides around the village. This was when the uniformed Hitlerjugend took action, making sure that the enemy pilot did not escape. Such excitement!

After one such incident, the Hitlerjugend Group held a young English pilot captive on the hillside, until some soldiers, from the elite SS detachment in Spree, arrived to take charge. The Group sang at the top of their voices as they descended into Spree. Tired but exhilarated, Hans decided on an early night, only to be soon awakened by a sudden brightness filling his bedroom, accompanied by the sounds of breaking glass and fire! Leaping from his bed, Hans rushed to the window to see Mr and Mrs Rosenbaum standing outside their shop with soldiers in the all black uniform of the SS. Their shop was on fire and Hans worried about Gretta but, knowing that the SS were there, he felt sure that all would be well. Mother and father came into his room and said that he must get back to sleep and that their house

BERLIN
Berlin-Tegel Airport
Charlottenburg Palace
Olympic Stadium
Congress Hall
Tiergarten Zoo
Europa Centre
Alexanderplatz
Museum Island
Brandenburg Gate
Sportforum
Spree
Berlin-Tempelhof Airport
Dahlem Museum
Botanical Garden
Free University of Berlin

was quite safe. When Hans asked what was happening, they replied, "We will explain in the morning."

A bleary-eyed, tousled-haired Hans emerged for breakfast, startled to find Gretta sitting at the table. As he took her hand in his, he noted that her eyes were red and full of tears. He looked at his father, who offered his work-roughened hands to them both. "Sit down, Hans, while Mother gets you some breakfast, and I will tell you what happened in the night. You know that Gretta's family do not attend our Lutheran Church on Sundays because they are of the Jewish religion," Otto continued, pausing to swallow heavily for he was obviously distressed. "Well, Herr Hitler has ordered that all people of the Jewish faith should be taken to special labour camps, where they will work for the betterment of Germany in these difficult times for us all."

"I expect our Führer recognises what wonderful workers the Jews are and is giving them this wonderful opportunity to work together for their adopted country," said Mother, arriving from the kitchen with three plates full of breakfast.

Gretta sobbed, "Why did they have to burn down our house?" and gripped the hands of Hans and Otto tightly.

"So that nobody could steal your father's possessions and business I suppose," Gerda answered, continuing, "You must stay here with us now Gretta, as I promised your parents before they left early this morning." This explanation seemed to satisfy the children for the moment and Hans suggested that he accompanied Gretta across the road to see what they could find of her clothes and personal possessions. The first thing they spotted painted across the burned-out shop were the words "Juden Raus" with the Star of David too, which made Gretta cry, as she leaned heavily on Hans' shoulder.

"Come on, Gretta, we will move you into the bedroom next to mine," Hans cooed, as he gave Gretta's shoulders a hug. "That would be nice," Gretta responded, noticeably more cheerful.

Otto and Gerda had decided that they would relieve any tension by concentrating on Hans' birthday party. Otto decided to enlist the help of boys of the Hitlerjugend Group to build the tree house, as a diversion after the trauma of the burning and Gerda involved Gretta in planning the refreshments and programme, for the same reason.

The postman brought a letter from Ernst, Jan and Heidi next morning, saying that they were looking forward to coming to Hans' party and, as there had been a lot of bombing in Berlin, how they welcomed the opportunity to stay in Spree for the night. So, once again, there were happy times ahead!

No sooner had Hans' cousins arrived, full of excitement both at the prospect of getting away from the air raids and of catching up on all the latest news in Spree, in the company of their favourite Uncle Otto, who was always full of stories of the forests and the creatures that lived in them, when there was a thundering and crashing in the east and shells started to land in the hillsides! Soldiers of the *Wehrmacht*, in their distinctive, grey uniforms, flooded into Spree, fully armed and with heavy artillery. Gerda and Gretta were hard at work treating soldiers with wounds, as the Russian army was advancing toward Berlin and causing many casualties, as the German army resisted them. Hans and some older members of the Hitlerjugend were told to hide their uniforms and lie low, until the battle had passed through Spree. Their turn would come to resist the enemy later. Thus his father cautioned him.

Gathering his cousins around him, Hans passed on this message. "They obviously want to capture Berlin," he said "and that is when we will fight." Ernst and Jan nodded vigorously, "So much for a quiet visit away from the air raids but our turn will come and we will be ready," they agreed, asking Hans to keep in touch with them.

Suddenly, there were German soldiers entering the house. First they took up positions at the windows, pointing the rifles down the main street. The sergeant ran upstairs with two men to do the same from there. The youngsters were excited, as they hid in the cupboard under the stairs, trying to keep quiet until Otto came looking for them. He put his finger to his lips, telling them to be quiet, as there were Russian soldiers right behind him! Crack went the sound of a gun, followed by Otto's body slumping into the cupboard onto the children! Otto Ludmeyer, the gentle forester, was the first resident of Spree to be killed in the war! Hans and his cousins resolved to resist the Russians when their time came!

The Russians entered all the houses in Spree, looting every scrap of food and fuel they could find. Gerda asked Hans to keep Gretta close to him at all times for the safety of the dark-haired, young beauty she was growing into. Hans readily agreed to this! Boys of the Jugend wanted to fight back but the elders of the church cautioned them that, for the moment, they must not meet and that their time would come to gain revenge. Hans and Gretta thought of the cousins often and vowed to make contact again in Berlin as soon as possible. In the meantime, Hans took up his father's duties in the forests, as he, too, loved the trees which now needed much surgery and care after the ravages of battle. Hans felt very close to his father working in the forests. There were no wages, of course, but they did not go without warmth, and there were the fruits and nuts of the forest to supplement their meagre diet. Gerda was pleased to have the company of Gretta while Hans was out. They found that they had a common interest in nursing the sick of the village and, with the doctor drafted into the army, there was always someone at their door in need of some liniment, a bandage or advice. The burned-out shell of her parents' home was a bitter reminder to Gretta of her hatred of war and she would talk to Hans about what they could do to help restore Germany.

Hans had grown tall, bronzed and muscular by the time Berlin surrendered and was divided into four zones of occupation, Russian, French, British and American. Hans could well understand why some of the Spree villagers tried to escape from the Russian zone into the British or American zones where life was more pleasant and food available. The Russians put up notices forbidding people to escape and there was a rumour that they planned to build a wall to prevent this happening!

"We must stay here, live as best we can and bide our time, Hans," Gretta cautioned Hans one evening, when he talked to her about a scheme he had in mind to escape from the Russian zone. "That is what your father would have advised," she added.

And so that spring and summer of 1945 passed into memory. Hans and Gretta consoled each other on the loss of their fathers. The war was over and the truth about the deportation of Jews became known. Gretta knew that she would never see her parents again. Hans burned his Hitlerjugend uniform in disgust. One day, returning from work, Hans told Gretta of a disused railway line he had found that ran through the forest. It had been built to transport timber to Berlin on low flat-bedded trolleys. "If we both got onto one of those at the top of the mountain, I think there would be enough momentum to carry us straight into Alexanderplatz, Berlin, where my cousins live. If I can get a message to them I am sure they will meet us and hide us in their home, which is just where the British and French sectors of Berlin meet, and we would be away from the Russians."

Gretta, who had been annoyed by the advances that young Russian officers had been making toward her, caught hold of Hans' arm in a hug. "If you think it would work Hans, I will come with you, of course."

Gerda had to be told and both of the youngsters spent several months stocking up with food, fuel, and medical supplies while Hans walked a section of the six or seven miles of track every day, clearing the line and looking for places where the trolley could possibly come off the rails. At home, they saved every scrap of grease from their food, which Hans took to work daily to smear on the wheels of the old trolley that he had cleaned up, ready for their escape.

Magically, one spring morning, Ernst, Jan, and Heidi arrived in Spree on their bicycles! "They have allowed us out to visit relations for the day but we must not stay too long," Heidi called out with a broad smile, as she saw her Aunt Gerda. Gretta was very happy, as she saw the parcels of food they had brought. "Is it good in your sector?" she asked. "Hans wants to talk to you about it, as he has a plan." The girls chatted away animatedly, as the boys set off into the forest to find Hans who looked up startled, as he pulled some bracken over the trolley he was working on. "I was just thinking of you and wondering how I could get in touch secretly because we are fed up with the way the Russians are treating us and I have a plan to escape!" Ernst and Jan were impressed with the trolley that Hans had restored like new and they listened intently as he unfolded his plan. "Brilliant," exclaimed Ernst, "I think it will work as the old line goes into a tunnel and into the forest at the top of our garden," Ernst continued, excited by the prospect of having Hans and Gretta joining them. Jan, a little older than the other two, said, "As long as we know what time and what day you will arrive, we can keep watch to see that no-one is there to stop you. We could even set up a diversion if anyone turned up." They all agreed that this was a good idea and set about calculating how far the journey was and how long it would take on the trolley downhill.

It was three lads flushed with excitement that came back to the house for tea. Hans winked at Gretta and then realised that they should outline their plan to his mother.

"Very good, you will need warm clothes and some sandwiches for the journey, and, Hans, you know about weather signs, choose a time when there will not be any ice or snow, which probably means anytime in the next two months." Before the cousins left on their cycles, day, date and time had been fixed. Gretta could share a room with Heidi and Hans with Ernst and Jan. "We can get extra food on the black market," the boys assured their aunt.

"When shall we go?" Gretta asked Hans every day for the next month. Hans, recognising his responsibility in this matter, spent at least an hour every day working on both the railway line and the trolley. Grease was the problem, as the insects and animals of the forest made a meal of it, as soon as he had smeared it on the axles of the trolley! Finally, after much discussion with his mother, Hans declared to Gretta that the weather was set fair and they could make the trip on Hans' sixteenth birthday, August fourteenth, which he had arranged with Ernst before they had parted in the Spring! At this decision Gerda and Gretta grew even closer, making provision and plans for the journey. "Don't worry, we will be fine and we will come back for you as soon as we can," Gretta called to Gerda, putting her arms round the older woman's shoulders, as they made parcels of spare clothing into cushions to take the bumps out of their ride.

August fourteenth dawned bright and the youngsters were up and tucking into the heartiest breakfast that Gerda could provide with the meagre rations available from the occupying Russian authorities. "We will do better than this next time we eat breakfast together, Mother," Hans said, continuing, "and that will be before Christmas too!"

The climb up the hill, deep into the forest, kept them all too breathless to talk until they arrived at the spot where Hans had hidden the trolley. He ran to it and pulled off the covering bracken with a flourish, "There Mother, doesn't that look good?" and Gretta, bending down to load the two children with their parcels, struggled to keep the tears from her eyes. "God bless you both," Gerda said softly, as she gave the trolley a push along the rails, to send them on their way to freedom.

The two young people clung to each other harder than they ever had before, as the trolley trundled at first and then gained speed as the incline grew steeper. The dappled sunlight on their bodies gave them warmth as they sped under a wonderful canopy of trees toward their destination. Gretta was comforted to feel Hans' strong, young body pressed to hers which, with the softness of the cushions fashioned from the spare clothes they had brought, gave them both a feeling of excitement, anticipation, and confidence in their mission.

The "clickety-clack" of wheels running smoothly over the rails, that Hans had laboriously greased and checked over for so many months, encouraged them to relax until, as expected, they entered the tunnel that they knew was nearly at the end of their journey. Hans gripped Gretta firmly, whispering in her ear, "Very soon we will run into the bales of hay that Ernst and Jan will have laid out to bring us to a stop." Gretta squeezed him in acknowledgement and they both smiled as they faced each other.

The "clickety-clack" slowed noticeably as the sweet smell of hay reached their nostrils and they came to a halt to cheering and the clapping of hands. Opening their eyes, they peered into the gloom of the tunnel, straight into the barrel of a rifle! Seeing Hans' startled look, Ernst pushed forward through the steel-helmeted soldiers and helped his cousins off the trolley. "All is well, Hans," Ernst called out, "these are British Tommies and are our new friends". Heidi appeared and helped Gretta tidy herself up after their journey. "Come down into the house for a wash and some breakfast and we will explain everything."

Aunt Marlene was laying out food on the table of her huge farmhouse kitchen as Heidi and Gretta emerged from the garden. "Welcome to Alexanderplatz and congratulations on your escape, Gretta. I have heard so much about you and Hans from Heidi and the boys." The two girls were soon upstairs in the bedroom that they were to share. Gretta stayed as long as she could in the hot bath Heidi ran, and the girls talked excitedly about their adventures and plans for the future.

"Come down for breakfast," Aunt Marlene called and there were wolf whistles from the boys, as the girls walked into the kitchen to find the three boys deep in conversation with four British soldiers, who had removed their steel helmets out of courtesy to their German hostess.

Ernst, who had assumed the role of head of the family after his father had been killed in France in 1940, stood up and called for quiet, as soon as everyone had been served breakfast. "I think I should make the introductions before we go any further," he said and continued to introduce Hans and Gretta, who had escaped from the East and would now be staying at the farm as part of the family. He turned to the soldiers and introduced them as "our new friends who have helped us to stay alive by bringing some of this delicious food we are eating this morning" and looking directly at the sergeant he continued "and this is Taffy Williams whom we are able to occasionally provide with some items that he and his men need." The soldiers roared with laughter at this, giving each other knowing nods and winks! Gretta, not quite understanding this, joined in the warmth of the laughter anyway, knowing that she was going to enjoy it here with her new family. But where was Ernst's father she wondered? She suddenly remembered that, perhaps, Hans and she were not the only ones to have lost a beloved parent during the five long years of war.

The party eventually broke up and it was time for private conversations as Aunt Marlene, having enquired about Gerda, "left on her own in the East", directed them all to their respective quarters, to make plans for the future.

Gretta and Hans went to school with their cousins the next morning, enjoying the comparative freedom of movement in the British zone of Berlin but horrified at the devastation of their once beautiful city. Life was good again and Hans wanted to contribute to their new good fortune. His opportunity came when Sergeant Taffy Williams arrived at the farmhouse, at the weekend, with a sack of potatoes and three large tins of what he called "bully-beef". Ernst, who had a particular interest in motorcars and anything mechanical, handed over to "Taffy" some heavy items wrapped in black, oily cloth, which he explained were engine parts that Taffy wanted and could not get easily to keep his platoon's vehicles running. "You see, Hans, the Russians are not only stopping food getting through to us Germans, but everything for West Berlin has to be flown in from Britain and even America at present." Hans shook his head in disbelief at this. "How can I help then Taffy, I can only get things that grow in the forests?"

"Well, my boyo," said Taffy at this news, "I do not have enough fuel to keep the boilers going in my unit and some wood could be very useful if you can get it."

This gave Hans plenty to think about. He wondered whether, if he pulled the trolley back through the woods at weekends, he could load it up with cut timber from the store he had always maintained since Otto had been killed, and, then, lying on top to hold it down, he could repeat the journey of his escape! He could also call in to see his mother! Gretta was worried about this scheme and suggested that he check it out with Aunt Marlene before doing anything. "I like the part where you can call in to see your mother, Hans," said Marlene "she must miss you terribly, and why not ask her if she would like to come back with you on the trolley one weekend, once you have tried out the scheme and found it feasible?" Reporting this to Gretta with great excitement they agreed that, after a few trial runs for timber and if Gerda wanted to join them, Hans would do it. "I will continue to learn English and attend the nursing classes at the International Red Cross as my contribution," Gretta blurted out, as she was very conscious of her good fortune, having lost her family in what was now called "The Holocaust".

"This has been the best Christmas for years," Gerda cried, as they cleared the table after a superb meal. "Let us raise our glasses to peace and absent friends," she continued sombrely, for, although she too loved her new Alexanderplatz family, she sorely missed Otto and her marital home in Spree. They all drank heartily the home-made cider to wash their dinner down, after which the five youngsters agreed to wash everything up while the two "aunts" took an afternoon nap.

Hans was doing well in school where he found a natural interest in botany and biology while Gretta furthered her knowledge of the English language and biology. She loved to practice her expertise in English when Taffy and his men came at the weekends.

After the traumatic time avoiding the occupying Russian soldiers and planning their great escape, Hans found his new-found and much appreciated security something of a routine bore. He discussed this with Ernst and Jan one time and they decided that they would get involved in the new political parties that were emerging in Germany. Gerda and Marlene, having seen what power politics had produced in the 1930s, were not happy about this idea, suggesting that the best way for the boys to help build a new Germany was for them to concentrate their energies on their education. And so it was that Hans and Ernst enrolled in two-year courses at college in Forestry and Motor Mechanics respectively, while Gretta concentrated on her nursing. However, there was much political turmoil over the dismantling of German factories and the struggle for power in the now divided Germany, and the boys enjoyed the lively, political debating society meetings at college! They both worked hard, as their mothers ensured that they were not distracted from their studies except for a game of football at the weekend. The two years passed very quickly. Examinations taken and passed saw two proud German mothers witness their sons receiving first class degrees in their chosen subjects. Gretta could not help remarking to Gerda after the ceremony, "Wouldn't his father have been proud?"

The first general election in a decade was called for August fourteenth, 1949 which happened to be Hans' twentieth birthday! Though more than a dozen parties were presenting candidates, the main battle was obviously going to be between the S.P.D. (Social Democrats) led by Kurt Schumacher and the C.D.U. (Christian Democrats, led by the ageing Konrad Adenauer. The two young men were caught up in the excitement of political campaigning, now that they had their professional qualifications. "We might as well take this opportunity to meet those who will be in power in the future and will become the employers of young chaps like us," they both agreed, as they looked for the main chance for both Germany and themselves!

The outcome of the election gave the C.D.U. the right to form the government and ensured that Herr Adenauer, now seventy-three years of age, would become Bundeskanzler, the first federal Prime Minister. Several ministerial offices were housed in the Bonn Natural History Museum. This was due to the devastation caused by wartime bombing. Each window had below it a medallion depicting a bird or animal of the forest. Hans, who had a great interest in the museum where he had found a job, amused his friends by telling them of how the Bundeskanzler got to be known as "the sly old fox", from the medallion of a beady-eyed fox below his window! Ernst, whose natural ability with the internal combustion engine had been invaluable to the C.D.U. during the election campaign, when he had kept whatever vehicles they could muster running, had been offered a job with Volkswagen, while Jan had been called into National Service in the new German army. Now there was money coming into the house in Alexanderplatz, food was readily available in the shops and life in Berlin was getting back to normal. After a good meal in the farmhouse kitchen, the entire family sat talking one Sunday. Gerda, who felt she had a special responsibility for Gretta, said, "Hans is going to the University of New Berlin to do a Ph.D. in Forestry, Ernst has an apprenticeship with his beloved motor-cars, and Jan is in the army. So they are all well occupied for the next few years. Now, Gretta, would you like to build a career in nursing, which we all know you love?" Gretta was a little startled at this because she had been thinking only about the washing up and the walk that she usually took with Hans after Sunday lunch! Hans, who felt he knew Gretta so well said, "Let's go for our walk and talk about it, Gretta, and you can see what plans Mother has when you have decided."

Hans was so happy, he felt he would burst, as he led Gretta into the tunnel where they had concluded their great escape. Sitting on a bale of hay he started to talk about something that had been on his mind for some time. "As I will be at university for the next four years, why don't you do what mother suggested and further a career in nursing, Gretta? Then, when we are both qualified, I think we should get married." Gretta's heart leapt at this and the couple embraced each other. "Oh yes, Hans, that would be wonderful. Let's hurry back to tell your mother and Aunt Marlene."

"This calls for a party!" Aunt Marlene said after Hans and Gretta announced their engagement and plans for the future. Heidi, Jan and Ernst had finished clearing away after lunch and were sitting in the drawing room enjoying the usual, after-meal conversations that had made their family so united. Hans and his mother often remarked on their good fortune to have come to Alexanderplatz, and all the more so because Gretta had joined them, completely recovered from the awful deportation of her parents to the extermination chambers.

Gerda sat with Gretta, discussing plans for her chosen profession. "There is a new hospital near the Botanical Garden, perhaps we can both go there to enquire of the work possibilities? I will ask Ernst to drive us into Berlin when he has a day off work." Gretta knew of the new hospital. They had both remarked how conveniently close to the University of Berlin it was, when she had gone to the Botanical Garden with Hans.

Experience with the International Red Cross, plus her good biology record from school and her natural role as a "carer" gained Gretta an offer as a trainee nurse at the hospital, where there were staff quarters too. Hans beamed at this news as he was going to live on the campus at university. "Our problems are over, my love. We will be able to meet in our spare time," he positively cooed to his sweetheart. "Yes, but our studies must come first, of course, and I must get to see Heidi frequently, as she will miss me now," Gretta responded.

Sunday afternoon walks down the *Unter den Linden* were a regular feature of life in Berlin, as Germany seemed to quickly recover from the ravages of war. The youngsters exchanged news of their respective week's events. Hans found the work hard. He had chosen "The reafforestation of Germany" as his thesis, concluding that there was a mountain of work and opportunity for him to achieve in this field, such had been the devastation of the forests. "My top priority will be the reafforestation of the Spree Valley, in memory of our fathers," he said to Gretta, as they walked arm in arm. She had a piece of news for Hans too, "Do you remember Sergeant Taffy Williams? Well, he had an accident, dropping an engine on his foot, and the British Army Medical people needed our facilities to attend to him. He came to the ward on which I was working and, because he taught me English, we had a good, long conversation. He, too, is looking forward to going home to his Valley, which he told me is so "wonderfully green". "What a coincidence," Hans exclaimed, "I really liked old Taffy."

And so, the betrothed couple enjoyed being away from home, meeting each other whenever they could, maintaining a rigid work discipline in their studies, whilst making time to get to Alexanderplatz to keep up with news of the family. Gerda, herself a natural carer, learned all she could about nursing from Gretta on these visits, while Hans would travel to Spree in Ernst's car, making plans for the reafforestation of the beautiful valley of his father. "One of the first things I will put in my plan will be to demolish the burned-out shell of Gretta's old home, where I will plant a tree garden of remembrance," Hans said earnestly to his cousin, who gave him a funny look, as he had not even noticed the superb, vintage Mercedes saloon that had just passed them!

Aunt Marlene held out a letter from Jan as the boys returned for tea. "He has been on exercises in Norway with British soldiers, and is thoroughly enjoying their comradeship too. So, perhaps we can now look forward to peace in Europe for a good long time now." Hans took Jan's address, saying, "I want to write to Jan to get him to find out about some strains of coniferous trees they have developed in Scandinavia." Ernst shrugged his shoulders!

The first two years of Hans' university course passed quickly and pleasantly. There were visits to Bonn and Cologne, where he was able to log the degree of destruction to forests throughout Germany. His research gave him great pleasure, using the Spree project as an example of what he could achieve overall if he could gain the funding for his project. "Funding is the problem, but I made some wealthy and powerful contacts when I dabbled in politics at college, and, afterwards, at the museum. When I have my doctorate in forestry, I will make sure that I get the funding!" Hans said to Gretta with conviction. "And then we will get married, and that is in about two year's time." Gretta hugged Hans, as she was so proud of his determination. "About then I should be a nursing sister too."

Thus, the ambitious plans of two fatherless, young Germans were laid and a 1955 wedding scheduled. Heidi was excited about the wedding plans and visited Gretta at her quarters in the hospital often. Hans' graduation ceremony saw all the family and friends attend. Gerda and Gretta were simply bursting with pride as he received his Doctorate from the Chancellor of the University, who remarked that "Hans was the first person ever to gain a doctorate in forestry, and, while Germany had young men of his stature, the future was in safe hands." Photographers took many photographs which duly appeared in the National Press. And, then, it was Gretta's turn to take the limelight, as she received her diploma as a nursing sister, in the presence of her adopted family. There was a surprise "congratulations" for her, as she descended from the stage, for this was spoken in English! Taffy Williams, always one to maintain "contacts", had heard that "little Gretta", whom he had first met covered in hay on an old timber trolley ten years ago, had made a success of her nursing career. Gretta, flushed with excitement, hugged Taffy, pulling him over to Hans, who suggested politely that Taffy should let go of his future bride! "When is the wedding then?" Taffy cried above the throng, receiving an answer and an invitation to attend in November. He promised to be there!

The newspaper photographs and reports of Hans' graduation brought a swift response! The Chancellor called Hans to his study a week later, "I have had a telephone call from the French *Ministre d'Interior* in Paris, Hans. They would like you to plan a scheme for the reafforestation of France." "But I am getting married in November," was all that Hans could think of to say, such was his elation at such a job offer. The Chancellor counselled Hans to take up their offer of an all expenses paid interview in Paris, to discuss the finer points of the position.

He telephoned Gretta and they decided that he must go on a fact-finding mission first, as this seemed either too good to be true or a gift from Heaven!

Fortunately, Gretta, Heidi, Gerda and Marlene had been working on the wedding plans for months and it was agreed that Hans should travel to Paris for the interview once he had authorised cousin Ernst, nominated to be his best man, to make decisions for him if needed.

"They have offered me freedom of planning and decision making, all the funding I need, plus a house on the outskirts of Paris for us, and the salary of a top executive to go with it!" Hans was really high, as he returned to the family home in Alexanderplatz. After Sunday lunch, the whole family sat in a discussion led by the two aunts. The only sad person was Heidi, who not only had not started on a career but was aghast at the thought of her best friend, Gretta, going to live in France. Gretta recognised this in her friend, taking her to one side, and comforting her with, "You will be my chief bridesmaid in three weeks time, Heidi, and you must come for holidays to us in Paris. Meanwhile, you must take my place with your Aunt Gerda and your mother, so there is plenty for you to do."

The day of the wedding was bright but cold. There were old school friends from Spree Valley, whom Hans questioned about how his forests were responding to his treatment plan. Taffy had rounded up a few of his platoon, who were still stationed in Germany and they reminisced around the huge kitchen table. It was altogether a very pleasant day, ending with Ernst driving the newlyweds to a Berlin Hotel in his company *Volkswagen*.

Addresses were exchanged and promises to keep in touch made, after which Gerda felt uneasy for it had not been without heartache for her beloved Otto that she had given up the responsibility for the two young ones, with whom she had been left. Marlene put her arm around her friend's shoulder, saying, "You have been talking about getting more involved with the International Red Cross, Gerda, now is the time, why don't we both do that starting next week?"

Mr and Mrs Hans Ludmeyer took a first-class train to Paris, marvelling at the continuous trail of devastation, only relieved by tracts of new factories, symbolising the rise of the new Germany. Dortmund, Essen, Dusseldorf, the heart of Germany's industrial Ruhr, learned about only in school, passed by the windows, as the newlyweds sped toward their destination. Clinging tightly to her arm,

Hans whispered to Gretta, "Remember the last time we were on a railway track together?" Gretta returned his embrace. "About 300 miles still to go, I estimate. Let's eat our lunch." They tucked into the sumptuous lunch basket that Gerda and Marlene had thrust at them as they boarded the train in Berlin.

Deliriously happy, full and content, they both fell asleep to the movement of the train, waking only momentarily to witness stops at cities plucked from school geography lessons.

Hans was the first to awake fully. "That must be the Seine down there," he whispered to his love, as the majesty of the Eiffel Tower was reflected in the noble river of Paris. A young man, holding a sign with "Ludmeyer" written on it, greeted them at the *Gare du Nord*. He spoke in stumbling German and led them to a taxi, which sped across bridges to a very grand-looking hotel close to*Notre Dame* Cathedral. "Hans had had two years of French in college and explained that Gretta could speak English if that would help. Much relieved, but puzzled that young Germans could speak English, their guide, Henri, having seen them into their room, explained that he would collect them after breakfast the next day, when they would meet the Minister and be taken to their new home.

"Let's have a wash and walk out to see *Notre Dame de Paris*, Gretta," Hans suggested for he could not wait to explore this legendary city. Gretta, who had established meal times and wanted to get their clothes out of suitcases and hanging in the spacious wardrobes, replied, "There are three hours until dinner, Hans. You go to *Notre Dame*. I will unpack, bathe, and dress for dinner."

They slept well that night, awaking fresh to absorb the great adventures lying ahead. True to his word, Henri was at the front desk after breakfast, greeting Gretta with an embarrassed "Good morning, Madame Ludmeyer." Blushing, Gretta replied in English, "Good morning, how are you?" To which Hans added, "*Comment ça va*?" Laughingly, they were taken to a brand-new motor car, which was going to be the car that went with Hans' new job! Hans looked at Gretta in amazement through a broad grin, as they were driven to the *Ministre d'Interieur*.

The Minister spoke fluent German, which was a relief to Hans. Whilst not going into details "at this stage", he explained, "Henri here will help you to settle into your new home. Report back here next

Monday to commence your duties." Kissing Gretta's hand, the Minister bade them both "farewell for the moment".

"Look at this kitchen, Hans, it is as big as Aunt Marlene's," Gretta cried in wonderment, as they inspected the large house that was to be their home for the ten years of Hans' contract with the French government. Henri, apologising for some obvious war damage to the building, explained that the house had been the headquarters for the SS in that region of Paris during the war but that repair work had been ordered and would be completed within the month. The mention of "SS" sent shivers through their spines, as they recalled that night in Spree when Gretta's parents had been taken away. The couple spent the rest of the day inspecting the house and grounds, only interrupted by Hans driving Henri back to work, returning with his company car to find Gretta scrubbing every surface in the kitchen clean!

"One of the first things we should do is to get all of the family here to help us get the house and gardens into shape," Gretta said when Hans returned. "Good idea, Gretta, Ernst will love the garage, where I see there is an old, German army staff car rusting away."

With Christmas only a few weeks away, it was decided that all of the family should come to Paris. "It will make a good holiday for them all and we have plenty of room," they agreed. Hans sent train tickets for Gerda, Marlene, Heidi, Jan and Ernst, promising that they would be collected at the *Gare du Nord* on arrival. Much feverish activity ensued. Hans was very managerial with the builders, insisting they cleared and tidied as they completed the repairs. "After all, we are now executives and have to become accustomed to having our instructions complied with," Hans advised his young wife, who had been wondering what she was going to do as Hans became increasingly involved in his project. "I wonder if they are in need of nurses here, Hans?" Gretta said, after the Christmas celebrations were over and their proud family had departed.

"I have other plans for your nursing skills, Gretta. I think we should plan a family, don't you?"

As expected, Hans was very busy with the job, which meant travelling all over France, inspecting damage to natural forests and making plans to repair, replace and for infilling as needed. Fortunately, Henri became his chauffeur and general assistant which meant that, when he was away from home, he only had to concentrate on the job in hand, returning to his office to make drawings to support his written plans and submissions for funding.

"I expect to start nursing in August," was how Gretta greeted Hans' return from one of his inspections! "Wonderful, it could be born on my birthday," Hans hugged his wife. "I will telephone Mother straightaway."

Gerda, like all prospective grandmothers around the world, was delighted with the news of the baby, particularly so, when Hans added that, if it was a boy, they wanted to call him Otto, and, if a girl, Gretta wanted "Rose" to remember her parents, the Rosenbaums.

Gerda had some news for the "Parisians", as she called them. Jan had left the army with a good gratuity, which he was putting into a garage that he would run in partnership with Ernst. "We are enjoying our work with the International Red Cross, too, and I will be checking up on the latest techniques on the care of babies now!" Gerda concluded the conversation with her son.

Gretta spent much time tending the gardens that spring and summer. Hans was away a lot, supervising the projects that he had initiated all over France. They had decided to ask Gerda, Heidi and Marlene to stay with them early in August, to be available for the baby's arrival. Heidi was pleased to be with her good friend Gretta at this time and confided in her that, now that she was working as secretary to Jan and Ernst in the garage, she was meeting some very attractive, young salesmen who called every day. This pleased her friend no end!

Otto was born on the twelfth of August 1956, a healthy eight pounds baby boy. Hans came by plane from the South of France to be with his family. After all the excitement had subsided, a family conference happened, when it was decided that it would be a lovely idea if Gerda stayed on with them. "Frankly, mother, Gretta really wants to get back to nursing and we would love to have you stay here permanently," Hans, having discussed this with Gretta beforehand, put to them all and agreement was reached.

Sad farewells were made but, with the suggestion that they all returned in November for Otto's church blessing and Gretta and Hans' first wedding anniversary, family happiness shone through again.

"What a good job I studied English with Taffy Williams, all those years ago in Alexanderplatz!" Gretta burst into the study where Hans was working. "Why dear?" he asked, raising his head reluctantly from the drawing board. "Well, they were concerned about my French at the hospital, but, when an English surgeon asked me a question, I was able to reply in English and I have been offered a Theatre Sister's position to start as soon as Gerda is confident with Otto."

The blessing and anniversary party served further to cement the family relationships. They were all delighted to learn of Gretta's new position, Heidi was courting a boy who had been at school with them in Alexanderplatz, and, at the garage, the boys now had a Volkswagen dealership. Hans saved his bombshell for last. "I have been asked to address a world conference in Vancouver, Canada, on "the conservation and cultivation of forests as a renewable resource." The boys gasped and shook his hand warmly. Gretta looked at Gerda saying, "What a good job I have you here, mother, as Hans will be gone for most of February and March next year." The National newspapers made much of Hans' departure to the world conference, claiming that, although he was German by birth, France had recognised his talent and, with the success of his reafforestation plans in France, so had the rest of the world! Hans even had a letter of "*Bonne Chance*" from President de Gaulle, their wartime hero!

The post-war explosion in the use of newsprint, due to the need for manufacturers to advertise their products widely, brought about a worldwide realisation that paper was made from a commodity that did not have an infinite supply. In short, there was a need to conserve and replace trees! Always a subject close to his heart, Hans relished the preparation of notes for his Canadian presentation. "I will be able to see the fantastic Redwood forests of North America too, Gretta," he said to his wife, who was engrossed in a copy of "The Nursing Times" from England to which she subscribed. "*Chacun à son goût*," she replied in French, not wishing to dampen her husband's enthusiasm for his pet subject.

It was springtime in Paris when Gretta drove to Orly airport to collect Hans. Otto was walking quite steadily, holding the hand of his grandmother. There was so much to catch up on, so many questions to ask, as Hans disembarked from a sleek aircraft with "Air France" emblazoned on its fuselage. There were presents for them all, of course, and the three enjoyed a long conversation after dinner and long into the evening. Gerda, pleased to have her successful son home, remarked how she saw Otto growing in his grandfather's likeness and praised her daughter-in-law's dedication to her chosen profession too, adding, "I have got her to address meetings of the Paris branch of the International Red Cross too."

Hans had a yearning to return to the Spree Valley, first to see Ernst and Jan in their motor dealership, and, secondly, to take his son to see the tree garden of remembrance he had built on the site of the old Rosenbaum home. "I think we should plant a bed of roses there too, to remember your family's surname," Hans, who had had this idea from a similar garden he had visited in Stanley Park, Vancouver, declared. "Mind you, it was overshadowed by thirty foot tall, carved, Indian totem poles but I think that that would be going too far!" he added, with a chuckle, taking his son into his father's beloved woods.

It was at Otto's first birthday party, with all of the family again in the big house in Paris, that Gretta announced that there could be another "Rose" in the family by their second wedding anniversary. She was expecting their second child in November!

The wine flowed freely as Gretta and Hans were congratulated. Heidi said that she would like to announce her engagement to Fritz, a boy from Spree. Gretta hugged her friend and proposed another toast, insisting that they spend their honeymoon in Paris. Aunt Marlene struggled to get a word in! "Fritz has a good job now and we have talked of the wedding early next year."

"Rose" was late arriving, upsetting Hans' well-laid plans for Christmas 1957! Gerda had everything ready in November but it was December tenth before Gretta declared she was in labour. Hans had been clearing up matters locally, now that he had completely ringed Paris with new or repaired forests, as a finale to end his ten year contract. With a busy family Christmas behind them, they settled down to plan their future. "We arrived in Paris as newlyweds with not a lot of experience, Gretta, and now we have two children, you are a respected theatre nursing sister, and I have started to become known on the international scene," Hans declared, obviously with much on his mind. "My contract finishes next summer and I will be out of a job, home and car, so I will be looking for another job. Perhaps we will go back to Spree?" Gretta was rather startled at this realisation, as she had grown accustomed to the good living they had enjoyed for the past decade. "I do not think that there is enough for us in Spree, Hans, do you? I think you had better see what else there is available in Europe."

Heidi's wedding to Fritz brought all the family together again. Otto was a pageboy and Gretta matron of honour. "We are going to miss this big house, Hans," Aunt Marlene sighed, when it was time to leave.

The leaves of the deciduous trees were falling in forests across Europe when television news carried the tragic story of how an old tip of waste materials from mine workings at Aberfan, South Wales, had slid into and engulfed a school full of children at their lessons. As parents themselves, Hans and Gretta watched these pictures with horror, little realising what significance to their lives this tragedy would ultimately have! Gretta resolved to send a letter of sympathy to Taffy Williams, now a grandfather of four children, with whom Ernst had always corresponded.

"At the office today, we were talking about Aberfan and their Welsh Office has decided that all of those old coal tips must be removed and trees planted to stabilise the ground," Hans said excitedly returning from work. "In fact, I had a telephone call from a British contact I had made at the Vancouver conference. He said that there is talk of a complete reafforestation programme for the whole of Wales, and I told him that I had finished here in France and was looking for a job!

Within a month, a letter arrived from "Forest Enterprise Wales" (F.E.W.), explaining that they had learned of Hans' work in the reafforestation of both Germany and France. They were establishing a "Valleys Forest Initiative" (V.F.I.), planning to combine successful timber production in the valleys of south Wales with the responsibilities for conservation, recreation and employment, to become one of that country's most successful prime industries, designed to have a huge multiplier impact on the Welsh economy and employment. "Would Herr Ludmeyer like to discuss the project with them?" the letter concluded.

"More upheaval," Gretta sobbed for she had enjoyed their time in France. "Why don't we drive over there for the interview, love?" Hans responded, half expecting opposition. "We could then go on from London, which we have both wanted to visit, driving into Wales, where we could perhaps see old Taffy," he continued, as he had given the matter a lot of thought. "The children can stay with mother and Marlene in Alexanderplatz, so we have no worries there either." They talked out the whole scenario long into the night, covering every subject from "where would we live" to Gretta's, "I hear that they have an excellent Health Service over there and I have seen job advertisements in my *Nursing Times* that I would have liked to apply for."

"Now we are getting somewhere," Hans whispered, as they turned to go to sleep curled in each other's arms.

With the children installed at the farmhouse, the plane to London Heathrow airport was touching down before they knew it. A hired car was waiting and the signposts to London were plentiful. A hotel room had been booked for them by the Welsh Office, which was only a short walk away down historic Whitehall. The Minister, offering a welcoming handshake, answered all of their questions, suggesting that, rather than driving to the Valleys, they took the train adding, "I will have a car and driver meet you at Cardiff General station."

"A few days to see London first," Hans suggested, anxious to make it a pleasurable visit for Gretta. Marble Arch was compared with Paris' *Arc de Triomphe* and like all first visitors to London, they had to see Buckingham Palace, Big Ben and St Paul's. A taxi to Paddington station and reserved seats on British Rail's "Intercity" express for Cardiff started the day well. Over coffee in the buffet car, a relaxed Gretta reminded Hans that "all of their new adventures started off with a train ride" "Spree to Berlin, Berlin to Paris, and now London to Cardiff," Hans took up, recognising the warmth of the moment.

"And how well they have turned out for us, Hans. We are very lucky people aren't we? And this next adventure will be just as good too, I am sure, as Wales, like Spree Valley, is very rural, which will be good for our children.

David Jones from the Welsh Office was there to meet them at Cardiff General Station. "It has been suggested that we go straight into the Rhondda Valley, which is at the heart of our Valleys Forest Initiative and where your office will be, if you decide to join us." The "Heritage Hotel", nestled in the heart of the Valley, adjacent to the redundant Lewis Merythr colliery, now recycled as "The Heritage Centre", was to be their lodging for the rest of the week. "I am to be your chauffeur and guide," David Jones advised them, adding, "The Minister would like you to see him again for your observations, when you return to London." Over lunch, David answered all of their questions. Hans was impressed to hear that there were 3,500 hectares of forest area in the Rhondda under Forest Enterprise ownership, of which thirty-seven per cent was under trees. Gretta asked, "Where should we live?" David told them of a brand new town that was planned on the mountain, adding with a smile "It is to be called "Newtown" too, and will be fifty per cent community and fifty per cent private housing. Let me drive you there. I assume you will want to buy your own house?"

"Newtown" impressed the Ludmeyers. Gretta selected a four-bedroomed house in a cul-de-sac and they fixed it up with the agent then and there, subject to financial terms to be arranged in London. Hans loved it too, as there was a superb view of some of the mainly coniferous forests, that had been planted in the 1920s to ensure a steady supply of pit props for local mines and to replenish depleted woods used in two World Wars. "It is so much like Spree Valley and they started my work seventy years ago!" said an incredulous Hans, as he tried to take it all in. Gretta felt at home too. "Remember how Taffy used to boast how green his valley was? I wonder if David could find him? I have his address here."

Taffy Williams was sitting by a roaring coal fire in his cottage on the hillside when his surprise visitors were shown in. "Dieu, Dieu, boyo, fantastic to see you, and Gretta, bach, you have not changed a bit since I was at your wedding in 1955, wasn't it," Taffy said in his lilting Welsh dialect. "Come down the club for a pint with the lads. We have a lot to talk about" Hans checked with David Jones, who was enjoying the reunion. They agreed to do as Taffy suggested but Hans insisted that they had only come to see "IS YOUR VALLEY STILL GREEN?"

The move into twenty-three Hann Close was effected quite smoothly. The house in Paris had been furnished, so there were only suitcases full of clothes and personal effects to have brought over. The Welsh Office co-ordinated everything for Hans and Gretta, who enjoyed searching for furnishings in the big stores of Cardiff and Newport. Taffy William had been a tower of strength, fixing curtains and all of the manual jobs that need doing on moving into a new house. Hans had thrown himself into his new job with a relish! "This is a far bigger job than I realised at first but, with the experience gained in France plus the helpful nature of my workforce, who really want to see their Valleys regenerated, I am going to enjoy our new life in Wales." Gretta smiled, happy for her husband, but she was missing the children and suggested that they telephone Gerda and Aunt Marlene to bring the children over at the earliest opportunity. "Don't worry, I will get my staff in the office to sort all of that out for the week after next. Then I can pick them up at the airport," Hans offered, continuing, "Why don't you phone home right now. They are in the same time zone as us." The doorbell rang and it was Taffy. "I have brought you some rhubarb from my allotment, Gretta, and now I am going to take your husband down to the "Owen Glendower" for a pint, as we have both been working hard and I want to start training him to be a Welshman!" The two friends strode off to the Owen, named after, as Taffy was proud to explain, a famous Welsh chieftain, who opposed the English King Henry the Fourth in the fifteenth century!

The children were now too old to play in the sand pit that Taffy had made for them in the garden! Marlene and Gerda were welcome female company for Gretta, who had soon mastered driving in the Welsh Valleys and was able to take them out sightseeing, while Taffy's daughter, Myfanwy, stayed with the children. "This is a real treat for me, Mama, as Hans is working so hard and enjoying everything so much that I am alone quite a lot," Gretta confided to her mother-in-law knowing that it would go no further. "Yes, I can understand that, Gretta, but I thought that you were going to continue nursing, which will get you out of the house, and doing what you enjoy," Gerda replied.

"Funnily enough, there was an article in the *Rhondda Leader* last week, about setting up a Cottage Hospital here in Newtown, quite small, of course, but I thought that that would be the very thing for me, as Otto and Rose could see to themselves after school until Hans gets home, or, in emergency, there is always Myfanwy to call upon."

Gerda looked with envy at her daughter-in-law, saying, "Why don't we enquire about it and look at the plans while Aunt Marlene and I are here?" Gretta agreed willingly, remembering what good friends they had become at the International Red Cross in Berlin, after the war.

"Somewhere different to go today, Aunt Marlene," Gretta called, as her aunt came down for breakfast. She was really enjoying having the company but taking them sightseeing every day wore a little thin. Now they could drive to the Community Health Centre offices in Ystrad to enquire about the new Cottage Hospital facility planned for

Newtown. Gretta gained an application form and details of where the site was, as well as what was planned to go there. "It sounds wonderful, Gretta, just an accident and emergency ward and another for maternity to start with, with plans for growth as the population expands," was Gerda's enthusiastic observation. Gretta felt the same, knowing that she had the qualifications to become an important member of the staff, yet to be appointed. "But I must talk to Hans about it first," she added, knowing that Hans, too, had ideas about getting involved in their new community.

Gerda was happily sitting with her grandchildren in the garden at Hann Close, when Hans arrived home from work and dinner was served. There was much to talk about! The ladies were due to return to Germany at the end of the week, and there was still a lot of Wales to see! Let's take the train to Porthcawl with the children tomorrow was one suggestion. Then Gretta mentioned about the Cottage Hospital and was delighted when Hans said that he was in favour of her taking up the job if offered. "But, ladies," Hans said, "there is something else I have thought of. It is our ruby wedding anniversary and I have booked a table for dinner for us all on Saturday, in that nice restaurant in Pontypridd."

Chapter Three
Guido

There was a great deal of unrest in 1930 among the young men living in the pleasant region of Amelia in Northern Italy. There was no work to be had due to a worldwide depression of trade. The Fascist dictator, Benito Mussolini had grand ideas of ousting Haile Selassie, the pleasant, little emperor of Abyssinia and had taken Italy into a war in Africa, recruiting an army from unwilling citizens, who found that they had problems enough feeding their families without feeding the megalomania of "*Il Duce*".

Augustus Sidoli and his friend Benjamino Bracchi walked into the big city of Bologna at the start of a particularly depressing week, when news had come through of a savage defeat of the Italian army with hundreds of casualties. "Perhaps that will stop the mad dictator now, just a shame about the men who have lost their lives," said Augustus. Benjamino nodded in agreement, adding, "Not that there are any jobs here for them anyway." Arriving in Bologna, they slaked their thirst at the fountain first, before walking to the newspaper offices where they hoped to find news of jobs. "Look at this Ben," cried Augustus excitedly, pointing to an article on the front page of the newspaper in the window of the printers. "Coal miners wanted to work in the booming coalfields of South Wales," he read quietly, leading Ben into the reading room. The two men read every word of the article, even though they did not really know where South Wales was, for they had a great need to work to earn money to keep their families fed and clothed.

The twenty-five mile walk back home passed in a flash it seemed, as the two men, deep in conversation, fired with hope, considered every angle and feasibility of this possible new opportunity. First they decided that they would ask the Priest where South Wales was, and the way to get there. "He is an educated man, and we can walk there," Gus said to Ben without conviction. After thinking this idea over, Ben, who sometimes cooked in the only restaurant in the village, added, "And we can get work picking crops and doing odd jobs on the way, sleeping under the stars." The two young men had decided that they would tell the members of the "Blackshirts" at their meeting that evening, and see if there were any others that would like to join them on this adventure. They were not happy with the programme of the Blackshirts, a political fascist organisation, set up only to further the ambitions of Il Duce. They were compelled to join the "Balilla" section for the under ten year old boys and, having enjoyed the camping and walking in the mountains, found that now, at over fifteen years, the "Fascista" section was cruel, selfish and highly military.

Aldo Carpenini called the meeting to attention for he was the sergeant for the evening. Corporal Berni stepped forward to inspect the men's uniforms, saluted, and stood them at ease. "Now, men, Ben and Gus have been to Bologna today and have come back with some exciting news to tell us all," the corporal said asking Augustus and Benjamino to take the floor. "Alfredo, will you get a circle of chairs laid out for us?" Gus asked the older of the two Fulgioni brothers.

The plan was formed at that meeting with Luigi Rabiotti, the son of the village café owner, agreeing to visit the Priest to work out a route to South Wales.

"Walk!" cried the Priest, "Well, I suppose it is possible, and, if there are six or seven strong, young men together you will be safe, as you will have to walk out of Italy, into and all the way through France, until you meet the English Channel." For, to the amazement of these uneducated, young Italians, South Wales was even beyond England! "I will get my books out and draw a map for you Luigi," concluded the Priest, thinking, 'They will need a map and the prayers of us all to achieve this goal.'

The families Sidoli, Rabiotti, Bracchi, Carpenini, Fulgioni and Berni had much to discuss that spring. The wives and mothers were fearful; the fathers and brothers wished that they could go too! The priest had calculated from the map he had drawn that they had roughly 1,500 miles to cover and had offered to write for guidance to the cardinal of the Roman Catholic church in South Wales. "You will need to get into training, get some fifty and hundred mile walks done and plan what you are going to take, as it all has to go on your backs, and you will need plenty of shoes!

Being members of the Blackshirts had trained the young men to work together and this time they believed in what they were doing!

Wiser heads took over as parents counselled their sons in an attempt to calm their excitement. "Give it a couple of years to see if things get any better here, and you will need that length of time to get into serious training," Papa Rabiotti advised one evening, when the lads met at his café after a meeting of the "Fascista". They could see that this made sense and, as they were already a uniformed team, decided that they would do the fifty and one hundred mile walks, that the Priest had recommended, under the guise of Blackshirt "exercises". Sergeant Aldo Carpenini offered to plan the first exercise, a seventy-five mile hike to Parma, where they would stay overnight, then a further seventy-five miles again to Milano!" Altogether that will be 300 miles there and back which, with our gear on our backs, should sort the men out from the boys!" Anxious glances were passed around but Carlo Fulgioni, always in the shadow of his older brother Alfredo, was the first to speak up. "Yes, I am for it because we are only kidding ourselves we can walk 1,500 miles, if we don't prove that we can walk 300 miles first!"

That decided it. A Quartermaster was appointed to plan what food and kit they would need. Gus and Ben agreed to work with Aldo on the route, while Luigi's father, who had brewed up a fresh pot of coffee while he was listening to the lads, appeared, with a broad grin on his face, saying, "Now you are talking sense and I think you will do it!"

With this encouragement, they enjoyed their coffee and decided that they would attempt the 300 mile round trip to Milano in June!

Feverish but organised activity filled the long, workless weeks. The small community searched for and repaired shoes that still had life in them. It was decided that each man would wear two sets of clothes on the trek to South Wales, washing the outer set when compatriots said so, they agreed with a loud laugh! The Priest spent a lot of time with his young parishioners, advising, directing and encouraging them in the enormity of the task they had set themselves. He could tell that there was a better feeling in the village, for now, through these brave, young men, there was, at last, a glimmer of hope for a better future.

Carlo Fulgioni was appointed to look after their meagre money resources for they all pooled what they could raise from family and friends and would add to this anything they could earn through casual work. The Priest took Carlo, who was one of the more literate of the group, to one side, offering him a notebook in which to record the movement of monies. "And, once a month, you must write to me to let us know where you are, and that you are safe and well. I will then tell all of your families, who will be worrying about you, of course."

The regular Friday meeting of the "Fascista" was buzzing with excitement! Sergeant Aldo Carpenini called his troop to order and asked for reports from Luigi, Gus and Ben on the route plan for the 300 mile walk to Milano and back, and from Carlo Fulgioni on his job as quartermaster and treasurer! By the time they had got to Papa Rabiotti's café for a drink, they were all keyed up for a June first start for their trial walk.

Arturo Sidoli held tightly to his two year old son Guido's hand, as they walked home from church. He had heard what his father Augustus was planning and feared that his son could lose a grandfather on such a crazy scheme. Augustus was deep in conversation with Mama, as they walked in the May sunshine. Mama seemed very happy and chatted merrily, so his fears were allayed for the moment.

The church bells rang, calling everyone to cheer the departure of seven strong, young men on their "trial" 300 mile adventure, that warm sunny morning on June first, 1930. The Priest firstly led them all in prayer, concluding his address with a vision of hope for all his parishioners and emphasising that they would hear of the hikers' progress from the pulpit, as letters written by "our dear, brave Carlo Fulgioni were received". Little Guido Sidoli clapped and cheered along with everyone else, as he watched his grandfather, Augustus, stride out in the June sunshine, only looking for his father's hand, when the cloud of dust raised had settled and everyone dispersed.

Father Andreotti decided that he would spend the rest of the day moving among his flock, reassuring them of his faith in their sons for he knew that this was a God-sent opportunity to restore hope and renew faith to them all. "We estimate that they will be home in September, God willing," the Priest said, giving parents some dimension to the hikers' task.

"They have made it to Parma!" Father Andreotti announced from the pulpit three weeks later, reading the first letter from Carlo which, he was delighted to see, was well written and detailed. "See, he says they are all well, sleeping in the fields and finding jobs for food on farms."

Buoyed by this, priest and parishioners alike found a new spring in their step as they set about their daily tasks. It was a month before there was any further news from Carlo, who explained that they simply could not afford the postage to write every week, adding that, "when we are walking for work in South Wales it will be different"!

Seizing on this note of confidence, the priest led his flock in prayer and thanks that Sunday. "They have reached Milano on schedule and, apart from some sore legs, are fine and will be home for the grape harvest next month."

What stories there were to tell when the seven returned! Guido accompanied his grandfather to Papa Rabiotti's café, where these now mature young men recounted the exploits of their three month test hike and made plans for "the big one", which they would start at Easter the next year.

The priest had taken to joining them at their planning meetings, as he felt a personal responsibility toward them. The letter from the cardinal of the Catholic church of Wales was full of both caution and encouragement to the young Italians whom he told that the valleys of South Wales were "green and hospitable" and that they should contact him at the Cathedral when they arrived in Cardiff. Father Andreotti produced a piece of white cloth sheeting on which he had drawn a map of their route. "Look, here is Cardiff and the Valleys that the Cardinal mentioned," Gus said, pointing at the map, which the eager young men studied.

"Now that you have proved that you can walk 300 miles, I have worked out what I think is your best route, avoiding some very high mountains which would be impossible for you to cross!" Father Andreotti interrupted their excited study of his map. "You will see that, as Genoa is about the same distance as Milano, I am suggesting that you make that your first target, then Turin, Lyons and Paris before the Channel, which separates France from England. And that is where you should ask for work on a fishing boat that will land its catch in England," the Priest concluded, realising the enormity of what he was suggesting.

The portly figure of Papa Rabiotti, arriving with a fresh pot of steaming coffee, interrupted their gasps of incredulity at what lay ahead of them. "Excuse me, Father" he said with a broad smile, continuing, "You and I have faith in these boys, and, with the Lord on their side, we know they will do it." The hot coffee and this vote of confidence gladdened the young men's hearts, as they resolved to have regular planning meetings every Friday until Good Friday, when they would set off for Genoa.

Papa Rabiotti agreed that they could use his café for their meetings and villagers began bringing shoes, socks, holdalls, and anything they thought might be of use for their village heroes' quest, which the Priest reassured them weekly was both feasible and for the good of them all.

The brothers, sisters, nephews, nieces, and all young people of the village of Cresso y Bardi listened enraptured at what their older relations were going to attempt and there was a regular attendance at meetings of the "Balilla" section of the under ten years "Blackshirts" organisation, where they built rafts on the nearby River Ceano. "I wonder why Father Andreotti did not suggest that the "Fascistas" built boats which they could then sail to South Wales in?" Guido called out to his friends, with all the naivety of an excited three year old. "Don't be silly Guido," Eugenia Bracchi replied, giving him a push into the river. "This river does not go all the way to South Wales!" Guido spluttered up the riverbank yelling, "Your grandfather would be too fat and sink a boat anyway, Eugenia!"

And so the next generation of young Italians learned and laughed and loved their families, vowing to learn all they could at school, particularly in geography, ready for when their turn came to help their family fortune.

The tiny church was packed to overflowing on Maundy Thursday when Father Andreotti planned an extra-special service, to wash the feet of the seven adventurers and ask God's blessing for their enterprise starting the very next day.

The bells rang out again, families hugged each other and tears were shed, before the Priest gave a final blessing and led his flock into church for the traditional Good Friday service and the hope of Cresso y Bardi left for Genoa on a journey, that was to take them an estimated one and a half years, to a green valley and hoped for prosperity in South Wales!

The Priest, with a catch in his throat, called out to Carlo Fulgioni, "We shall be waiting for your letters!" All seven turned and raised a gentle wave of the hand in response.

Easter week was a traditional week of church and prayer and this year of 1932 saw additional fervour added to the congregation's prayers. The Priest assured everyone that he would broadcast Carlo Fulgioni's progress reports from the pulpit, as soon as they were received.

It was June before Father Andreotti had news that they had reached Genoa and were enjoying bathing in the water in the Gulf of Genoa, where they had found work, mending fishing nets. They were all in good spirits and ready for the next stage over mountains to Turino.

Carlo Fulgioni did as the Priest had asked him and his letters chronicling the party's progress arrived regularly, every month, describing their adventures, work, trials, and tribulations as 1932 unfolded.

Father Dino Andreotti gained great satisfaction from the work that he had put into encouraging his young parishioners to fulfil their ambitious undertaking, noting that there was a spin-off in that his church was full to overflowing on the Sunday that he had said he would read the latest newsletter! There was a noticeable improvement in morale in the village after each episode of news for they all, young and old alike, knew that their relatives were doing this for them, and, as there was little else to bring hope into their lives, Father Dino was well supported when he gave prayers of thanks to the Almighty.

"We worked in the vineyards in Asti for two whole weeks before arriving in Turino, where we have now found accommodation on a dairy farm," was the July newsletter's travelogue. Guido Sidoli and the "Balilla" group thought that they would practise some long walks to see what it was like, turning back on the second day when it rained!

Blistered feet were becoming an increasing problem after the long trek to Lyons in France. "But Aldo Carpenini went looking for work on the barges on the River Saône and has got us a ride north toward Paris, if we work our way there. That will be like a holiday for us all too," was the contents of the November newsletter, which brought a cheer from the congregation and pats on the back for Aldo's proud parents. The children dashed off to the River Ceano to play on their rafts with great glee.

Paris was a harsh, inhospitable, big city, where there was much unemployment and suspicion of a gang of young Italians looking for work, Carlo reported adding that, "as it was very cold, they were sleeping in the sewers which was not as bad as it sounds". Springtime in Paris put a whole new complexion on the scene, Luigi Rabiotti got a job in a café on the Champs-Elysées, after he explained that his father owned a café in Italy. Ben Bracchi soon joined Luigi there, so the whole party ate well until Easter which, unbelievably, meant that they had been travelling for a whole year!

Great celebrations were enjoyed both in the village and Paris at this realisation, Father Dino excelling himself with the fervour of prayers of thanks in which he led his flock.

"Now we head for the coast at Calais," declared Ricardo Berni, who still saw himself as "corporal" of his platoon!

"*Señor y Señora* Arturo Sidoli are requested to speak to Guido's teacher at the school, on Tuesday May 5th, 1933 at twelve noon" was the content of a piece of paper that Guido gave to his mother, as he arrived home from school one afternoon.

"At least it is all flat, without those darned hills that caused us so much grief getting into Lyons," Ricardo Berni declared, as they enjoyed the walk toward the sea in the cool spring air. "Yes, and I am sure I can smell the salt sea air like it was in Genoa," Augustus Sidoli nodded to his best friend Ben Bracchi in response, for the mood of the party was one of high spirits and optimism, borne out of the success of their adventure so far.

"I am rather concerned about Guido and his attitude to school work," the teacher started their interview, as the Sidolis sat nervously awaiting the worst! "He is a bright, energetic boy, more interested in adventurous games than reading, writing and arithmetic, which is a shame because he has a good brain, if only we can get him to concentrate for long enough." The Sidolis looked at each other, Arturo winking at his wife, as they thanked the teacher for her advice and walked home arm in arm. "I have an idea that I think will concentrate Guido's mind," Arturo said, continuing, "You know how he follows the newsletters about his grandfather's great adventure every month and sometimes enacts their exploits here in the village? Well, I am going to suggest that he learns to read Carlo Fulgioni's letters with Father Dino, and learns to write, so that he will be able to write to his grandfather, when they have an address in South Wales, which the Priest says will be later on this year, God willing!" Rosina Sidoli squeezed her husband's hand in approval saying, "I will suggest to Eugenia Bracchi that she works with Guido on this, as they get on very well together and she will be a good influence on him."

The smell of the sea led the adventurers to the harbour, at Calais, where a host of fishing boats were moored. Fishermen mending their nets prompted Alfredo Fulgioni to enquire if they could help, based on their experience in Genoa. Derricks were swinging great baskets full of wriggling, silver fish out to where men loaded them on to tables for women to prepare for market. This intense activity welcomed the Italian men's offer to work free, save for a working passage to England!

"They have arrived in England!" was the jubilant announcement from the pulpit, as Father Dino held Carlo Fulgioni's latest newsletter aloft. When the unseemly cheer subsided, the entire congregation knelt in prayer at this news.

After delivering the lesson in "Faith", the Priest took the hands of Guido Sidoli and Eugenia Bracchi and lead them to their "lessons" in reading and writing about their grandfathers' adventures in foreign lands.

Jean Claude Duvalier, skipper of the fishing boat that had accepted the offer of a free crew, was pleased with their work and thought of an idea of how to use these strong, young Italians again, to their mutual advantage. "Alfredo, you say that your next destination is London? Would you take this catch on the train to London's Billingsgate fish market if I paid your fares? That would mean that I could get a quick turnaround out of Folkestone harbour and back to Calais on the early tide." Alfredo shook Jean Claude's hand firmly and went to tell his friends of this extreme good fortune, as they unloaded the day's catch onto the quayside. "That will give you something extra to write to Father Dino about, Carlo," he said slapping his young brother on the back.

"They have been in trouble with the police in London!" Father Dino announced, dramatically, from the pulpit, continuing, "They had a job, to deliver fish to the London fish market, and found themselves so hungry that they stopped to cook some in a field that was really a city park and a London policeman told them off and made them move out of the park!" Carlo, wanting to tell of the wondrous sights of London, skipped on to tell how they had asked the policeman where the Catholic church was, had explained their need to the Priest, who had given them clear directions of how to get to Cardiff. “It is one great, long, straight road west now, first to Bath, where there is the Abbey, then to Gloucester Cathedral, where we are bound to get help, and then on to Cardiff Cathedral, where the cardinal has already been told about us by Father Dino,” Carlo concluded.

Augustus Sidoli, striding out on this “Great West Road” called out to his comrades, “To think that it was three years ago that we did that first trial walk to Parma and Milano, and it is now the same distance from here to South Wales!” For he had observed it was June first, 1933. They were all bucked up at this thought, as doubts had entered their minds since their stock of shoes was causing concern. “I think we can call this the last leg now, Gus?” Ben Bracchi questioned, as he caught up with his friend.” I wonder why they call it Bath? we could all certainly do with a good bath after that fish, couldn’t we?” This caused a laugh and raised the spirits of seven tired, tanned, young men who resolved to visit the Catholic church for advice on this matter as soon as they got to Bath.

The curate eyed them with a suspicion that turned to respect, when he heard what they had achieved so far. Fortunately, the young curate was of Italian birth and, for the first time in three years, they were able to recount the story of their journey and its purpose with some fluency. “Come with me to the Priest and I will tell him what you have told me and I am sure that he will want to help you. But, first, come to my quarters where you can bathe,” Peter, the curate, offered, leading the way. “Walk from Italy to South Wales!” Father Ryan exclaimed, having listened quietly, while Peter explained their presence in beautiful English. Tea with scones, cream and jam was soon served by the housekeeper, obviously eyeing these foreigners with great suspicion. They were invited to sleep in a storeroom and Father Ryan suggested that his curate might like to show them the splendours of Georgian Bath with its Roman history.

Carlo Fulgioni enjoyed the intellectual conversation of Peter and a firm friendship formed between the two men, who were of a similar age, as they walked through the wondrous history of the city.

“Father, would you allow me to accompany our guests on their walk to Cardiff through Gloucester?” the curate asked his superior, when he had exhausted his tour of the City. “I wish that I were young enough to come with you, Peter, and your English will be of great use to them," was the Priest's immediate response.

Father Ryan took "Faith, Endurance and Endeavour" as his text the next Sunday, having asked the young Italians to take up the front pews of his rather large church, so that he could tell the story of their success through the application of these virtues. He concluded, by asking the congregation to bring any men's shoes, that had life left in their soles, to church next week. "In the meantime, my friends, you must speak only English, which is also the language of the Valleys of Wales," Father Ryan advised.

Well-rested, well-fed, and well-shod, eight young men set off for Gloucester, where there was a bridge across the water to Wales, Peter had explained to Carlo, whose command of English improved daily, as the two walked side by side deep in conversation.

Guido Sidoli soon tired of learning to write, but loved to read the adventures detailed in letters from Carlo Fulgioni. "Come, let us light a fire and cook fish over it like they did in London," he suggested at a meeting of the Balilla. An excited "yes" greeted this idea from the other four year olds at the meeting, while Eugenia Bracchi stated that she "would ask Mama how to prepare and cook the fish properly". The long, hot days of summer soon passed in the village until, one Sunday in September, Father Dino was clutching a letter, as he climbed into the pulpit as the bells rang out from the belfry high above.

"They have arrived in South Wales," he announced joyously, as he observed the beaming faces of his congregation, who sank to their knees as he led them in prayer. "They have not been able to get work yet, though, as times are still very hard for the miners of the Rhondda Valley, who are not happy to have immigrants trying to take jobs away from them. But they have rented a house to stay in while they settle down." The congregation groaned at this news, which gave father Dino the opportunity to remind them of the value of faith "which has seen our boys tackle and achieve the seemingly impossible".

"That is it!" Guido announced, when they returned home. Startled, Arturo raised an inquisitive stare. "I will really get down to some hard work at school now, so that I can get a good job when I am your age, Dad." Arturo nodded his approval adding, "If Uncle Carlo can not only walk to South Wales but also learn to speak English on

Sid with Ma and Pop Warner and Laddie, 1940.

Sid searches for coal on the slag-heap, 1940.

Marjorie and Sid dance at the rink, 1948.

Marjorie and Sid as they are now.

the way, you can surely learn to read and write well in our own language, Guido."

Luigi Rabiotti soon came up with an idea to earn enough to pay the rent on the house. "My father's café was started in the front parlour of our house back home, the kitchen was where both the family and customers' meals were cooked, and we all slept upstairs. We could do the same here, as we are almost on the corner of the street where the locals do their shopping, so we could put a sign out." Ben Bracchi, who had worked in cafés at home and in Paris, nodded vigorously and it was agreed that Carlo would look into getting supplies and all of the bookwork involved. Spirits were lifted considerably at this as the seemingly continuous rain, that the locals said was necessary to keep the mountains of the Valley green, plus the daily trudge to the pithead to ask for work, was depressing them all.

Ben Bracchi and Gus Sidoli scrubbed, cleaned and painted the parlour, while Luigi worked with Carlo on the limited fare they were likely to offer. "Bracchi's Café" was the sign painted on the front window, where Carlo had fixed his simple handwritten bill of fare. Every scrap of furniture from the house had been gathered together in the parlour, cleaned and repaired to accommodate their hoped-for customers who were already peering through the window at what was going on inside! "Cup of tea and a rock cake for tuppence please," was their first order, never to be forgotten, that wet Saturday morning!

"We have taken five pounds on our first day," Carlo Fulgioni announced to them all as they sat for their evening meal, cooked by his older brother Alfredo. Ricardo Berni, enjoying the traditional Italian meal of pasta, looked up at Alfredo with, "It looks as if this could be the answer, Alfredo, with your cooking and my brains. Let's look for another house to rent and do the same, shall we?"

"Britain at War!" the headlines screamed from the *South Wales Echo*, as the Prime Minister, Neville Chamberlain, explained that he had not been able to gain agreement to stop the growth of Fascist aggression in Europe. "Let's hope that Italy does not get into this war too" was the consensus of opinion among the new Welsh/Italian businessmen, who were enjoying life among their neighbours and customers in the green Rhondda Valley, where they had discovered a common interest in singing and Aldo Carpenini was now a respected tenor in the male voice choir.

The waters of the River Ceano at Cresso y Bardi village still flowed, as families gathered for summer picnics after church and children playing happily on the water's edge, as their elders discussed the latest progress report from their absent loved ones in South Wales. The arming of "Fascista" units of the Blackshirts was cause for great concern, as it seemed that "Il Duce" was bent on joining his German friend, Adolf Hitler, in an attempt to conquer all of Europe! Arturo and Rosina Sidoli joined the Bracchi family for a glass of wine, as they watched Guido and Eugenia play at "cafés", imitating the actions of their grandfather's progress, that Father Dino had just reported from the latest newsletter from Carlo Fulgioni.

"How happy life could be for us all in that green valley," grandmother Sidoli sighed, watching Guido growing in the likeness of his father and her beloved Augustus, so very far away. Arturo put his arm round his mother's shoulder whispering "perhaps some day", for he too missed his father of whom he was so very proud and, every time some money was sent, he ensured that his now quite literate son, Guido, wrote to his grandfather and uncle Benjamino Bracchi in acknowledgement. "Here's to Bracchi and Sidoli," Rosina announced with a raised glass, lifting the nostalgia she sensed creeping into the happiness of the two close families.

Italy entered the war in 1940 and all citizens of Germany and Italy were "interned", which meant that the movements of the proprietors of the now three Bracchi's were restricted and they had to report to the police station every Friday at 10 a.m.

"It could be worse," they all agreed, as they decided to adapt their already meagre bill of fare to the restrictions imposed by food rationing. "The Welsh love their fish and chips, so, if we can't get fish from Cardiff and Barry docks, let's see what else we can cook up to go with their chips," was a positive suggestion by Aldo Carpenini at a "war conference" which the young restaurateurs held. Various ideas for the making of "pasties" was suggested, after a list of available ingredients had been drawn up, and the three cafés with their young proprietors became a welcome place to visit, as the Welsh went about their daily lives. The men worked long hours in the mines and tended their allotments, enjoying fresh air and producing vegetables, when off shift, while their womenfolk cleaned, scrubbed, sewed and knitted, as their contribution to the wartime difficulties that had been imposed on them.

The restrictions imposed by warfare were seen in air raids on Cardiff, Newport and Barry Docks and the shortage of supplies. All mail from home was suspended too, creating a feeling of isolation which was countered by immersion in local affairs. Aldo encouraged others to join the male voice choir, while Ben and Gus found an outlet in the Rhondda Chamber of Commerce where their "potato patties and chips" were the talk of the Chamber, producing remarks like "only the Italians would have the nerve to coat a slice of potato in batter, fry it and serve it up with chips, for fourpence!"

The end of hostilities saw several of the now prosperous restaurateurs married to pretty, young Welsh waitresses who had caught their eye and starting families of their own. Bracchi's cafés had opened in all of the Rhondda from Pontypridd, Porth and Pentre to Tonyrefail, Tonypandy and Treherbert, with a reputation for good food, well-served and at reasonable prices in spotlessly clean surroundings.

"Why don't we go in for ice cream, too?" Augustus Sidoli asked his friend and partner, Ben Bracchi, as food supplies became more readily available, in spite of there still being some rationing.

Carlo Fulgioni, now secretary and book-keeper to them all, resumed correspondence with Father Dino back home where, after some fierce fighting had caused damage in Cresso y Bardi, things were getting back to normal again. "Young Guido is a chip off the old block, Gus!" Carlo announced, as he burst into the big Pontypridd restaurant one morning, clutching the latest letter from Father Dino Andreotti. Going on to explain that Guido Sidoli was now the manager of Papa Rabiotti's café, which he had helped to rebuild after the war damage. This news pleased Augustus, who had been reading of the prowess of Italian ice cream in the trade magazine *The Caterer* and toying with the idea of an exploratory visit home where he could also see his beloved wife. Ben Bracchi could see the logic in such a visit, as his acute business sense assured him that the British were anxious for anything in the dessert line, after five years of bland "rations".

"I think a visit could be cost-effective, Gus," he said, as they drove back to Porth from the wholesalers. "Why don't we get Carlo to cost out a trip for us and we'll see," was Augustus' cautious response.

The decision was soon taken out of their hands, when a beautifully handwritten invitation to the wedding of Guido Sidoli to Eugenia Bracchi, in July 1950, arrived, with a letter from their grandchildren, explaining that they were going to live over "Rabiotti's", in which they now had a share.

Great jubilation was engendered by this news and a "council of war" discussion, over several bottles of Chianti, concluded that Gus and Ben should not only fly home for the wedding but research the importation of ice cream for sale in their now seven Bracchi's cafés, for each of the now not so young Italian immigrants had set up his own business, taking the style and name of their first joint café, where they had all slept over the top!

Carlo Fulgioni, as secretary and book-keeper for all of the Bracchis, agreed to sort out the "paperwork" relating to the proposed visit. Passports were applied for and the help of the local Thomas Cook's travel agency sought and gained. Alfredo Fulgioni, jealous but proud of his young brother's grasp of the language and business acumen, offered to drive Ben and Gus to Rhoose, Cardiff's International Airport, in good time for their flight to Milano. "Remember to drive on the other side of the road," was but one of the many messages, jokes and pieces of advice they had been offered, to take with them to their beloved village of Cresso y Bardi!

When Father Dino brought the letter, accepting the wedding invitation and with details of the proposed travel plans, to Arturo and Rosina Sidoli, Arturo, who had learned to drive in the army asked his prospering son, Guido, to loan him his car so that he could collect his father from Milan International. "And you can take Grandma with you too, Papa," Guido suggested, knowing that his father's ageing mother was somewhat bewildered by what was happening!"

The church bells rang out as they had not rung since seven young men from the village had left on their desperate journey of hope! Father Dino had orchestrated the return of two of his sons, so that maximum impact was gained. The tiny church was filled to overflowing with people and flowers, the six families Sidoli, Rabiotti, Bracchi, Carpenini, Berni and Fulgioni, all dressed in their best, occupying the choir stalls. Guido and Eugenia watched outside for Ricardo Sidoli to arrive in the car, dashing to the church door to signal to Father Dino first, then back to hug their grandfathers and lead them by the hand into the church, where the entire congregation fell to their knees as the Priest led them in prayers of thanks.

Guido was invited to mount the steps to the pulpit, from where he invited everyone to Rabiotti's café for a buffet meal, so that the families, whose sons were still in Wales, could meet and talk to the two village heroes. The excited chatter and general confusion was just too much for Grandma Sidoli, so Eugenia took her to sit in the shade of a tree, bringing Augustus to sit by her, as soon as she could drag him away from the throng. Guido moved smoothly among the crowd, laughing here, shaking hands there, very much the young businessman, as his admiring grandfather pointed out to Arturo and Rosina. Ben Bracchi gathered Eugenia and Guido to him for a private chat as soon as he was able. "Now tell me all about this fine restaurant you have here, Guido. Perhaps I can get some new ideas from you to use in our cafés in the green, green Valleys of Wales, where all seven of us Cresso y Bardi boys have made good business."

Startled by this and very much in awe of the two elderly visitors, Guido spluttered, "In fact, I am just investigating going into ice cream." Ben called his old friend, Gus, over to him at this, saying, "Here Gus, listen to what your grandson has just told me. He is a real chip off the old block!"

Little work was done for the rest of the week, as the two old gentlemen from South Wales were invited to take meals with the parents of their colleagues left behind. "Well, someone has to look after the businesses after all!" they laughed, dispensing the gifts that had been sent and receiving gifts to be taken back to Wales for their own particular family hero, with thanks for the cash gifts that had been forthcoming from that source over the years, as prosperity had evolved.

The day of the wedding of Eugenia Bracchi to Guido Sidoli dawned bright and clear and the entire village was invited! The church bells rang from 11 o'clock until everyone had left for a reception "fit for a Caesar", as Ben and Gus had ordered, which was served in two white marquees set up on the banks of the River Ceano. Music and dancing continued until the early hours, when the ageing visitors, with an early return flight to catch in the morning, sneaked reluctantly to their beds. Guido and Eugenia insisted that they drove them to the airport this time, stating, "After all, grandfathers, we owe you everything, and this is the least we can do, as you walked to Milano last time!"

It was raining in Wales when Alfredo Carpenini collected them at the airport. "And that is why our valleys are so green," he asserted, in response to their implied criticism. "Business has been good while you have been away and Carlo says that he has found a good place in Llantrisant for us to open our eighth café, but we will have a "council of war" tonight, hear all of your news from home first and then we can talk about business."

"Welcome back to the grandfathers-in-law!" "Corporal" Berni announced, as their jet-lagged friends entered the large dining room in the Pontypridd café. Laughter soon subsided when Ben and Gus explained how they had decided to report back to their friends. The two had concluded that, as there was so much to tell, they would share it among them equally. Benjamino Bracchi leaned on the back of a chair and told of their flying experience, their greeting in the village, the wedding, and of the gifts from relatives that they had brought back. Augustus Sidoli interrupted, "And we will tell you all the news of your families as we bring their gifts around to you over the next week," adding, "We had to buy another suitcase to bring them all in too! But let me tell you about young Guido, my grandson, now a restaurateur himself, he has developed a recipe for "Sidoli Gelata" which, knowing how the Welsh love ice cream, we are going to sell in our restaurants, once Carlo has looked at the figures." Luigi Rabiotti walked in with a tray of glasses of wine at this stage and the conversation flowed, with each of the other five soaking up every word from "home" until Ben and Gus declared that they "just had to get to bed".

Carlo Fulgioni was back in Pontypridd, where Ben and Gus shared an apartment over the restaurant, early next morning for he had matters of great importance to talk over with the two senior partners. Taking up a cup of coffee, he aroused them both, suggesting that they should have a "working breakfast", as he wanted to explore the possibilities of "Sidoli Gelati". The restaurant staff served "full Welsh breakfasts" to the three partners, who declared that they preferred this to the Italian style continental breakfast, washed down with wine! Ben Bracchi, sensing Carlo's excitement, invited him to "say his piece", at which Carlo enthused over a shop in the High

Street in Llantrisant, that had no competition nearby and of which they could buy the freehold at a very reasonable price.

"I have discussed it with our solicitor, who has said that, as we will now have eight businesses and own the properties, it is time for us to become a Limited Company, to protect our personal interests now that some of us are married with families. He also suggests that we should have an accountant to do all of the paperwork that I have done up till now! An accountant would save us more in tax than what he charges for doing the books." Gus Sidoli was quite amazed at all of this coming from Carlo, who was surely only self-educated? "You sound like my Guido, who, I am sure, would agree with what has been suggested," Gus complimented Carlo. "Now let me give you the figures on the manufacture and sale of our own ice cream," Carlo interrupted, as the waitresses cleared the tables, and the partners agreed that they should have a long discussion with their solicitor in Tonypandy.

"Fix it up for the day after tomorrow, Carlo, as we must get to the cash-and-carry this afternoon," Ben declared, rising wearily from the table.

All seven partners attended the meeting with the Solicitor, for there had been some grumbles among them regarding share of profits and workloads and "Corporal" Berni suggested "It is time that we got ourselves properly organised, just like Father Dino organised us for our walk here more than twenty years ago. That was a success but Ben and Gus have just found a better way! We have built up good businesses from nothing but hard work so, perhaps, there is a better way for us there too."

"The name "Bracchi" is synonymous with Italian-run cafés in the Welsh Valleys and I suggest that you form a Limited Company Bracchi's Company Limited, even though that is not the name of you all." John Llewelyn, the solicitor opened his address to the partners with these words, noting a general nod of approval from them all to this, and continued, "You will all be equal directors but will need to appoint a Managing Director, secretary and, I suggest, an accountant. There is Mr Jack Howells, in the offices next door to me here whom I can recommend as a very reliable accountant. Perhaps Mr Carlo Fulgioni would like to make an appointment to see him with your accounts?"

It was unanimously agreed that Benjamino Bracchi should be Managing Director "as his name was over all of the eight cafés" and Augustus Sidoli, Sales Director, with special responsibility for the manufacture, delivery and sales of Sidoli ice cream throughout. Naturally, Carlo Fulgioni was elected Company Secretary, to collect and bank all takings every Monday, as well as keeping the "day book" at each outlet, registering daily takings, purchases etc. Carlo enjoyed working with Jack Howells, learning something new and growing in stature and confidence every day. He still wrote to Father Dino every month, although now they occasionally had a conversation on the telephone with news exchanged more quickly and, through his visits to Jack Howell's office, soon learned of the wonders of the fax machine! Father Dino insisted that "he wanted nothing of such newfangled nonsense", giving Carlo Guido's fax number "in case of emergency".

Bracchi Company Limited prospered under the new system of control. Augustus, relishing his "Sales Director" title, brought in Sidoli ice cream, meeting the highest standards of the Health and Hygiene Authorities and running a competition for the most sales every month, with the director in charge of the winning café receiving £100 cash to reward his staff. "Because, after all, we all get the same wages now and they need the motivation," Gus had explained. This created some rivalry between the outlets, as well as keeping the staff interested and on their toes, resulting in the continued prosperity of the cafés that were now able to consider expanding into full-blown restaurants, ploughing company profits back.

The 1970s and 1980s saw the company grow out of all recognition, with new restaurants opening up in other valleys as far as Merthyr Tydfil, Abertillery and Ebbw Vale. Pontypridd was used as the training centre for young Welsh managers, recruited from those who had worked in the cafés already and proven their loyalty to the company.

Regular board meetings were now held, replacing the former "councils of war". The growth of fast-food hamburger chain stores was noted, along with the Chinese, Kebab and Curry house restaurants, none of which dramatically affected the turnover in the Bracchis, now a well-established part of the South Wales social and leisure scene.

"Augustus Sidoli, Sales Director of Bracchi Company Limited, appointed Chairman of the Rhondda Chamber of Commerce" was the headline in the *Rhondda Leader*, over an article outlining the growth of the company and its romantic history. The article went on to consider the way in which new immigrants now arriving from former British Colonies could learn from the successful integration of the Italians.

Carlo Fulgioni sent the article to Father Dino!

John Morgan's alarm clock awoke him at half past six in the morning in his terraced Newport, Gwent, home. "Cup of tea, love?" called his wife Megan who had spotted that it was a cold morning, with an unusually heavy fall of snow overnight, and wanted her man to go off to work with a good breakfast inside him. In here, Megan," John called from the bathroom where he was already shaved. "See you tonight about seven and we will go down the club for bingo," John answered, in response to his wife's farewell kiss and advice to "take care". Scraping the ice off the windscreen, John was relieved when his Cortina started first time and he was soon pulling into the gates of the "Cymru Carriage Company", where he had worked since leaving school. His lorry was loaded up with the engine turning over, as he picked up his list of deliveries to be made that Tuesday. The Transport office advised that all roads were passable on his route but care should be taken. "As always," John called out with a wave of his hand, confident in the knowledge that he had never had an accident in all of his forty years with "C.C.C."

First stop Caerleon, then Usk and Pontypool, with a final call in Abercynon, where he could get a hot meal in their canteen! "Red Dragon Radio" was switched on and he was on his way, soon recognising that there were patches of black ice on the smaller roads that had not seen early morning traffic yet.

"That was the Ebbw Vale police on the phone, Ben," Augustus announced to his friend, taking tea into the bedroom. Ben awoke with a start, demanding more information. Sitting on the end of the bed, Gus explained that the telephone ringing downstairs had awoken him and the Ebbw Vale police explained that they had been called to the café, where Islwyn Watkins, their Manager, had been charged with assaulting his wife after a domestic dispute. She had rushed out into the snow, knocking over a paraffin stove that had set the premises alight! "Nobody is harmed but the police would like to see the owners as soon as possible," Gus concluded. At which they agreed that they would wash and dress and get on their way. "If we take the transit-van we can go to the cash and carry in Abertillery on the way back," Ben suggested as his brain got into gear. Gus responded, "I hope the heater is working in the van as it is freezing outside."

Pontypridd to Ebbw Vale is about thirty miles, so we should be there in under an hour they agreed, as Gus took the wheel. They made deep ruts in the layer of overnight snow, as they pulled out of the parking area behind the café. Fortunately, the transit had been in for its regular service and M.O.T. test, so the heater and wiper blades performed perfectly as the two old gentlemen, deep in conversation, headed for the unknown. "Islwyn always had a violent temper, let's hope their children are okay, although the police said that nobody was harmed, didn't they?" Discussing what lay ahead the two partners soon found themselves entering the busy little town of Ebbw Vale. A small group of sightseers, huddled against the cold, stood outside the badly burned café, where the sign for "Sidoli's Italian ice cream" jutted out from the "Bracchi's" fascia board. Pushing through the knot of people toward a ruddy-faced policeman, stamping his feet in the doorway, the two men identified themselves as the owners of the premises and were asked to "pop round to the station and ask for Sergeant Davies", which they were pleased to do, having checked the contents of the till which appeared unharmed.

They were reassured that all of the Watkins family were quite safe and staying with relations, except for Islwyn whom they had taken into custody "pending the outcome of our investigations you see, Sir," Sergeant Davies had advised them.

"We might as well get off to Abertillery where, at least, we can get some hot coffee in the cash and carry and then home for breakfast, when we can phone our solicitor and get him to sort out the insurance claim," the two friends agreed, climbing stiffly back into the Ford Transit. Fifteen minutes later, they pulled into the newly cleared car park and gathered up a trolley, which they proceeded to load with eight paper sacks of potatoes, three five-gallon drums of cooking oil, sugar, flour, butter and cases of the soft drinks, that were popular with their youngest customers, with a packet of crisps after going to the cinema. Ben paid the bill, as Gus wheeled the trolley to the van and started loading up. "We have got a good load here, Ben," Gus said, as his friend appeared. "Yes, so the day will not be wasted and, as long as everyone is okay, we can let the police and the insurance company sort it out," Ben replied, as they climbed into their seats.

However, it was not easy to dismiss the matter from their minds as they drove off on the A467 again. "I can feel we have a good load up, Ben, but the roads are clearing nicely now that a little bit of sun is out." Each settled back in the warmth of the van's heater, their thoughts elsewhere, as they pondered over the happenings of the morning. As he applied the brake at the Crumlin crossroads, Gus felt the wheels of the van take over from him, as they went into a sideways skid that led them into the path of a large articulated lorry with the letters "C.C.C." emblazoned on its side.

Rabiotti's restaurant was crowded with Friday morning shoppers in the village of Cresso y Bardi in the pleasant Amelia region of Italy. A "peep, peep, peep" called Guido Sidoli to the fax machine in his office.

The letter heading was "John Llewelyn, Solicitor" Tonypandy and the message read.

"Regret to advise that on Tuesday, January 13th, 1982, Messrs Augustus Sidoli and Benjamino Bracchi were involved in a fatal road traffic accident. Funeral arranged for 11 a.m. Friday, January 23rd. Please telephone for further details. Yours sincerely, John Llewelyn, on behalf of Mr Carlo Fulgioni."

Guido, already working flat out, felt his heart come into his throat and made himself sit with a large coffee, while he absorbed the contents of this message. He knew that Eugenia was busy bathing their second child, Vittoria, and little Ben would be playing with his friends in the yard behind the restaurant. Guido, almost unable to control his tears, finished his coffee and gathered up two further cups on a tray, climbing the stairs to their living quarters. "Look, 'Tor, here is our lovely Daddy with a coffee for Mama," Eugenia said, looking up from the bath, perturbed when she saw her usually cheerful, smiling husband's grim expression. Guido could not speak; he simply put the tray by Eugenia's side, wrapped his sweet-smelling daughter in a towel and sat down.

Eugenia, always strong in times of crisis, read the fax, sipped her coffee and looked up at her beloved husband. "We must go straight round to your mother and father and then to *Nona* Bracchi," Eugenia announced, with a tremor in her voice, for she knew that she must support Guido at this time. In the short walk to Arturo and Rosina Sidoli's home, they agreed that they, the youngest members of the family, must make the decisions. Apart from *Nona* Bracchi, all other members of the family had perished in the war. Guido passed the fax to his mother and father, quickly translating the contents into Italian for they had both taken lessons in English so that they could correspond with their respective grandfathers and "uncles" in Great Britain.

The family hugged each other, gaining strength and support from this physical contact, as the awful news sank in. Guido took control, "We must all go round to *Nona* Bracchi now and then I will telephone Mr John Llewelyn on Monday and get him to answer all the questions we are asking ourselves right now." *Nona* Bracchi claimed that she had had a premonition that something had happened to her Benjamino. The youngsters said nothing but Eugenia comforted her grandmother as best she could, by placing her great-granddaughter into her arms, bringing a serenity to the old lady's work-worn and weather-beaten face.

Guido's mind raced for the rest of Friday. Fortunately, they had built a loyal and willing staff around them and the young Sidolis planned to fly to South Wales for the funeral the next week. Realising that Nona would not wish to make the journey, they booked four seats on the Air Italia flight to Cardiff International departing eleven o'clock a.m. Wednesday.

That done, Guido faxed the solicitor back asking that one of their "uncles" meet them and arrange hotel accommodation, concluding, "will telephone Monday".

Guido and Arturo Sidoli, Alfredo and Carlo Fulgioni, Aldo Carpenini, Luigi Rabiotti and Ricardo Berni were joined by Islwyn Watkins, as they waited for the two black hearses to draw up outside the Pontypridd Catholic church, stepping forward to bear the coffins of their friends. A fine rain watered the flower-laden coffins. Eugenia noted a wreath from a "John Morris of C.C.C", as she followed them into the packed church, such was the stature of the two Italian immigrants.

A finger buffet and coffee had been prepared in the big dining room of the Pontypridd restaurant, a short walk from the church. Strained conversations took place throughout, as friends from miles apart tried to catch up on decades past. Solicitor, John Llewelyn, moved inconspicuously among the throng, finally making a beeline for Guido, whom he addressed, "Will you, your wife and parents meet with me here, tomorrow, at three o'clock please? I need to discuss the contents of the will with you." Guido, still emotionally disturbed from shouldering his grandfather's coffin, nodded in agreement, taking Eugenia's hand and passing the message on. "Saturday will be busy in the restaurant, so can we please meet at the New Inn hotel where we are staying?" Guido pleaded with the solicitor through tear-stained lips. "Fine, sir" was the response.

"To Mrs Eugenia Sidoli (née Bracchi) I bequeath my fourteen per cent share in Bracchi's Company Limited and all my worldly goods" was the brief content of Benjamino Bracchi's will, matched by a similar bequest to Guido from Augustus Sidoli's will. John Llewelyn withdrew from the room to allow the family time for private discussion, promising to order coffee and return. Arturo Sidoli choked back the tears and cried "Dear God, they deserved better than this after all of that long walk and work!" Guido taking control, having had but a moment to think, said, "I have a plan. This means that Eugenia and I have a twenty-eight per cent controlling interest in the company and will need to be here to run it. I suggest that you, Mama and Papa, take over and run Rabiotti's back home, that Eugenia goes back with you and then brings the children here to South Wales, where we can live in that big apartment here in Pontypridd." The family, delighted to have a clear path ahead outlined for them, burst into excited chatter, with Eugenia casting the final vote with "Remember how they both talked at our wedding about their green, green valley? Well, now we will have the time to find out 'IS MY VALLEY STILL GREEN'"

Guido's plan was accepted by the family, his father and mother relishing the thought of running Rabiotti's. Final messages were exchanged, Eugenia returned to her children, leaving Guido to take up the reins as Managing Director, Bracchi's Company Limited.

Chapter Four

Yoko

The school bell sounded the end of the day's work for Yoko Yamamoto in his home town of Hitachi, seventy-five kilometres south-west of Tokyo.

Yoko was the first to close his books, bow his head to signify "Sayonara" to his teacher and dash out to where his bike was stacked along with every other student's, in the shade of the north side of the school.

"Dash" was all Yoko could think of because, today, his father, Claude, was to leave and take up his commission as a pilot in the Imperial Japanese air force and Nana-San, his grandmother, was giving a special party to celebrate her son's departure to the war. Yoko had been instructed to get home in good time to wash the street dust off beforehand. It had been a long, dry and dusty summer in this part of Japan. The fields were dry and the rains would not start until the sea winds changed and the south westerlies brought welcome relief from across the wide Pacific Ocean.

On arriving home, Yoko parked his cycle alongside his sister's and dashed into the small yard at the back of the home he shared with his mother, father, grandmother and sister.

Yoko loved his dad who rose at half past five every day, to cycle the fifty kilometres to Tsukiji, the great Tokyo fish market where, as a worker skilled in the age-old techniques of making Kamamboko, the spicy fish sausage, he was respected as a man of honour, courage, and total reliability in the Association of Sushi Suppliers.

How Yoko and his father enjoyed their weekends together when Claude, having bathed away the all pervading smell of the fish market, would lead his team of twenty-four "Fuji-walkers" into the foothills of the dominant Mount Fuji, for their weekly trek. Claude and his son would talk of the beauty of their countryside, honesty, trust and his loyalty and passion for their country.

Aisha was two years younger than Yoko, small in stature but always determined to keep up with the boys of the Fuji-walkers. She had organised a guard of honour to line the street for her father's departure. "Help me set out the tables, Yoko," Aisha called to her brother, seeing Nana-San carrying laden trays from the house. "What a feast we will have, look, there is horse mackerel to cook over charcoal and dishes of sushi, enough to feed the entire Imperial Japanese air force!"

The Yamamoto family savoured every moment during the twilight of this day. Food and laughter had always been a hallmark of the family and, although tinged with sadness that Claude was leaving them, there was the pride that he was going to serve his Imperial Majesty, Hirohito, and their cherished land. On the stroke of seven o'clock, excited chatter announced the arrival of the Fuji-walkers who, under the direction of Aisha, formed a double column and saluted military-style, as Claude, having hugged his family, left for the railway station and adventures that he had promised to relay in letters and on his return.

It was very quiet at home without Dad. Yoko missed hearing his father get up early and joining him for an early breakfast drink. Aisha, too, missed the stories of past glories of the Japanese Empire that Claude would tell them both before tucking them into their beds at night. She heard the grown-ups talking about a war that was going on in Europe, which Nana-San had explained was a long, long way away. Yoko, still only ten years old, took over from his father with the Fuji-walkers, planning exciting games for each weekend outing. He divided them into two teams of twelve or "armies", with the names of "Germans" and "Americans", that he heard on the Radio Tokyo broadcasts of the war in Europe. And so, on Saturday mornings, they would meet in the town square and devise a war game between the two armies. Yoko led the German army, who were trying to free all of the countries of Europe from slavery, while his best pal, Egochi, led the American army who, with the English, were trying to stop them. Great fun was had as they manoeuvred from side to side and up and down the gentle slopes of their beloved Mount Fujiyama. Another team of Fuji-walkers from the next village, hearing what great fun this was, asked Yoko if they could join in. Listening carefully to Radio

Tokyo, Yoko heard that the Italians had joined in to help the Germans and that the hated Russians were fighting on the side of the Americans and British. What a war was going on! And how these young Japanese enjoyed acting out their fantasy wars each weekend!

Captain Claude Yamamoto gave plenty of interesting news for Yoko to pass over to the Fuji-walkers in his weekly letters. How proud Yoko was, when he heard that his Dad had volunteered to be a Kamikaze pilot prepared to give his life for the Emperor and the glory of Japan. Yoko asked all of his "army" to give the same undertaking, as they swore their oath of allegiance to Mount Fuji and Japan. "Why don't *WE* join in the war?" The lads would ask but Aisha, who had formed a team of nurses replied, "Don't be silly. We must keep things going here at home, producing food and supplies, just in case the Emperor does decide to help the Germans and the Italians."

The south westerly winds brought in the autumn rain to help the crops of rice and wheat to survive, be harvested and stored for the winter. Aisha made sure that the boys' "armies" knew all about being prepared for a real war for, as she told them, there was more to fighting for your country than listening to the radio on Fridays and then playing at war at weekends on the mountain!

On Sunday, December seventh, 1941, there was much sounding of car horns and people cheering in the streets. Yoko got up from his bed to find out what the excitement was. On the early morning radio there had been the news that not only had Japan joined in the war with Germany and Italy but wave upon wave of the Imperial Japanese Air Force bombers had attacked Pearl Harbour and all naval and military activities on the island of Oahu, principal American base in the Hawaiian Islands, destroying the entire American Pacific fleet!

Monday morning saw a tired but exhilarated Yoko calling on his friends to walk to school. "Isn't school a boring nuisance when we could be up on our mountain fighting the Americans now that war has been declared?" Yoko said to Inu, a somewhat weedy lad, whose father worked in the fish market. "Yes," Inu replied, adding, "My Dad is going to join the Imperial Japanese army when they set up a recruiting station in the village."

Shaping their fingers as guns, the two boys shot and killed American, British and Russians from the trees, as they were joined by other children caught up in the excitement of being at war at last. School really was boring that day and they had a hard job concentrating on their books for arithmetic and literature in particular, but when it came to the history lesson, the teacher, reading their mood, chose a period from the wars that had built the mighty Japanese Empire. The door of the classroom opened and the school secretary looked in and beckoning the teacher over, she whispered something to her. "Close your books and pay attention, children," said the teacher. "Yoko Yamamoto, you are dismissed for the day and must go straight home to your mother." There was a buzz in the classroom as Yoko, startled, rose and left, his heart pounding. There were no enemy soldiers to be seen on his way home, Yoko noticed with a smirk. "That will teach them to take on the Japanese," he thought. Soon his home came into view and his pace quickened, as he saw his mother and Nana-San on the verandah, crying. "What is the matter?" Yoko said, with the words catching in his throat, as he saw that Nana-San was holding a piece of paper. His mother was the first to speak. "We have a letter from his Imperial Majesty, the Emperor, telling us that father was killed in the raid on Pearl Harbour, where he died the death of a true samurai warrior in the service of his country."

Clasping each other tightly, the three members of the Yamamoto family cried until Nana-San called them to prayer for the soul and spirit of their personal hero.

Yoko was the centre of attention at the next meeting of the Fuji-walkers. He had done a lot of thinking since learning of his father's heroic death and was determined to carry on with his work with the group of young people. "Why don't we set up a shrine to your Dad?" was a suggestion that Yoko had hoped to hear. And so, all weekend, they walked over their majestic Fujiyama, remembering that it was not only the highest mountain in Japan at 3776 metres above sea level, but was also a dormant volcano, that had not erupted since November twenty-fourth, 1707 which, the boys realised, by an amazing coincidence, was the day and month of Claude Yamamoto's birth! That decided it, they agreed, we will set up a shrine on the mountain! "Yes, but where? let's investigate."

By now they had reached the cone-shaped crater, some 2000 feet in diameter at the apex of the mountain and looked down the southern slopes to the shore of Segura Bay and the blue, blue waters of the Pacific Ocean.

"We had best ask the priest how to set about building a shrine to Yamamoto-San," said Egochi who, being sixteen, had become the

Honolulu Star-Bulletin, December 7th 1941

Honolulu Star-Bulletin 1st EXTRA

WAR!

(Associated Press by Transpacific Telephone)

SAN FRANCISCO, Dec. 7.–President Roosevelt announced this morning that Japanese planes had attacked Manila and Pearl Harbor.

OAHU BOMBED BY JAPANESE PLANES

general in charge of their Japanese "army". He turned to Yoko and asked, "Will you and Aisha come with me to the temple tomorrow morning?" They agreed and gained an interview with the priest of the Hitachi Buddhist temple, who explained that, although Yamamoto-San was of the Shinto faith, they were correct to come to him because Shinto was the rural faith of country people that had preceded the Buddhist faith in the sixth century. "I have an idea," said the priest, after a few moments of deep thought. "At Ise there are two wonderful Shinto shrines. Why don't you go and get some ideas from there?" "I would write to the Kami in charge at Ise and make an appointment first, if I were you," said the priest. Egochi looked at the other two and, thanking the priest, suggested that they would investigate the matter further.

"It is all very well for him to say go to Ise, but that is a full day's bike ride or more. When would we go and where could we stay overnight?" Yoko felt a bit down at this but, not being able to sleep that night, thought of his father and how he would have advised them.

The early morning sun streamed into Yoko's bedroom, heralding another glorious Japanese day. He could see the way ahead clearly now. They would form two teams, four boys and four girls, all of whom had or could borrow bicycles. They would ask for food from their mothers and take those two tents, that Claude had shown them how to use on the Fuji-walkers' trips to the crater. They would cycle to Ise on Kenkoku Kinembi, National Foundation Day holiday Friday, February eleventh, by which time the deep winter snow would have gone. They would make camp and cook at Ise, visit the Kami by appointment on the Saturday and cycle home on the Sunday. Yoko could not contain himself. He quickly washed and dressed and ran to Egochi's home to put the plan to him.

"Great idea," said Egochi, "I would like you, Inu and Akao in my team. Why don't you ask your sister to get three girls to make up a team with her? We will call a planning meeting at the weekend."

The Fuji-walkers met as usual at the weekend and, after an hour-long trek up the hillside, Egochi called a halt and asked everyone to sit down, when he told them of the plan to build a shrine to Yamamoto-San, their discussion with the priest and what was suggested. "I have asked Yoko, Inu and Akao to come with me to Ise and Aisha has asked Meija, Hoki and Niku to accompany her. We will set out on our bicycles on National Foundation day, which is a Friday, and we have made an appointment to see the Kami in charge of the two Shinto shrines at Ise on the Saturday. We will camp over the two nights as Yamamoto-San taught us and be back on Sunday evening with the plans ready. The rest of you can help by telling your parents what we are going to do to honour the memory of our hero, as we will need everyone's help to raise the money to buy the materials needed and then to get them to the site we have selected, overlooking Segura Bay.

Everyone turned out to see them off on their great adventure to Ise. The younger ones wished they could go too. Egochi called out to them, "Your turn will come; there is plenty for all of us to do!" The eight adventurers, cycles piled high with kit, pedalled off toward Tokyo. The excitement they all felt as they approached the big city! Soon, Yoko spotted a sign for "Tsukiji", "That is where my Dad used to work in the Great Tokyo Fish Market," he said. "Why don't we go there and tell the Association of Sushi Suppliers what we are doing?" This was readily agreed, as the whole journey was going to be the adventure of a lifetime, and soon they were in a stream of three-wheeled, motorised vehicles carrying stacked cases of fish. "These are called ta-rays," Yoko said, knowledgeably, as his father had told him about them. Arriving at the entrance to the Market, Meija, a pretty girl with protruding teeth, spotted a notice that said "Association of Sushi Suppliers" pointing up a flight of stairs. Egochi led the way, and pulling Yoko with him, he said, "Come on Yoko, what was your dad's boss's name?"

Climbing the stairs, Yoko knocked timorously on the door and, getting no response, turned the handle and entered a dimly-lit room filled with the pungent smell of fish. Yoko looked at Aisha who had followed her brother. "Get out of here, you kids," cried an old man, who was smoking a cigarette as he leaned over a candle-lit desk. Yoko walked over and offered his hand to the old man. "We are Yoko and Aisha Yamamoto and our father worked here for many years before joining the Imperial Japanese Air Force."

"I knew Claude well," said the old man. "I heard that he died a hero's death at Pearl Harbour, is that correct?" "Yes, Sir," said Aisha, who had been told to respect her elders, "and we are on our way to the Shinto shrine at Ise, where the Kami is going to tell us how we can build a shrine on Fujiyama to our father."

"Well done," said the old man. "You are going to need provisions aren't you? Here, take this box of fish and I see there are more of you waiting outside, so have these loaves of bread as well." "Thank you very much" said Yoko. "May we call on you again on our way back on Sunday to let you know how we have got on?" "Please do," said the old man, "your father was a very respected man at Tsukiji. Sunday is my day off but, as it is the Kenkoko Kinembi holiday weekend, why don't you and your friends call at my house at about noon for lunch?" Thrilled with this kindness from a friend of his father, Yoko shook the old man's hand saying, "Thank you so much, Sir, that will make our return journey so much easier." "Off you go now, young Yamamotos, I must get these books finished before the next delivery of tuna gets here from Osaka. My home is the one on the corner over the road. See you on Sunday."

Yoko could not wait to get back to their friends to show them the food they had been given and to tell them about the invitation to Sunday lunch. "Yamamoto-San was as well respected by adults as by ourselves," said Egochi. "Come, let us get on." And so, eight excited youngsters pedalled away with a warm glow in their hearts. Disaster struck, as the pedals of Meija and Niku's cycles clashed as they turned a corner! The girls fell on the worn, cobbled road and their knees opened up and red blood oozed from the cuts. Egochi, who had studied first-aid in the Fuji-walkers and thought he was in love with Meija, yelled for everyone to stop, as he dragged his first-aid box from his saddlebag. Aisha ran over to the accident with him and quickly attended to rearranging the girl's clothing modestly. "See if you can get me a bucket of water, Aisha," said Egochi, as he sorted out lint, antiseptic cream and bandages from his kit.

Meija started to cry and Egochi took her in his arms to comfort her. When Aisha said, "Leave this to me now Egochi. Why don't you take a look at their bikes to see if they are okay", Egochi shrugged his shoulders and walked off with hands in pockets. There was no damage to the machines and soon they were ready to leave. Inu, a studious lad, said, "We must be very careful now as not only is it getting dark but there will be a lot of holiday traffic on the roads." "I agree, and we need to find a place to camp for the night pretty soon too, so let's call at the next homestead we pass," interrupted Yoko, who was feeling that too much of his authority was being stolen from him!

Aisha called the girls to come with her to look for a place to stay that night and, at the very next crossroads, there was a pretty homestead, with cows in the fields and surrounded by trees covered in cherry blossom. She could have swooned it was so idyllic! "Look, you stay here and tell the boys that I have gone to ask if we can camp here tonight," said Aisha, leaning her cycle against a hedge. By the time the boys had arrived, Aisha was back, with a big smile all over her face! "Great luck," she cried," they are Fuji-walkers, too, and have said we can use their barn. Come, I will show you."

Eight tired but happy youngsters wheeled their cycles to the barn, which was full of hay. Deciding not to bother with the tents, they laid out their blankets as directed by Aisha, who said meaningfully, "Boys over there and girls here *and no peeping*"! Within an hour all that could be heard was the heavy breathing of the eight sleepers.

Aisha did not sleep well that night, conscious of her responsibility for her girls. However, the fatigue of the day took over and she awoke to a banging on the metal door of the shed and the cry of their hosts, "Time to get up! You can wash in the trough in the yard, where there is tea and breakfast for you all."

A fragrance of cherry blossom filled the air, wafted on a gentle breeze around the courtyard of the homestead. "It is a lovely day," said Aisha, as she gathered her girls around her to wash away the dust of the hay barn and the sleep from their eyes. Facing them was a long table, with a steaming jug of green tea at one end and an array of Kaiseki Ryori, the traditional Japanese multi-course feast of fish and vegetables. There was a clear soup, raw, fried and even boiled fish, with a mountain of rice and a dish of pickles. "Fantastic," cried the girls, as the boys wandered sleepily from the barn. "Wash first," Meija called to Egochi, pointing toward the trough and, in a moment, the boys were all hungrily digging into the food. Their hosts then appeared, with great bowls of fresh fruit as dessert, and much conversation ensued.

Yoko led them all in applause to their hosts as they wheeled their cycles out of the homestead. "Goodbye and thank you," they all cried, bowing low, as their hosts waved goodbye with a promise to "see you next year", when they had agreed to bring their troop of Fuji-walkers to Hitachi to see the shrine to Yamamoto-San.

Back to the slog again but they were eight happy, full and contented young people, knowing that today they would reach the Shinto shrines at Ise, their destination!

Soon they found themselves on the end of a carnival procession, a band at the head followed by colourful floats of every description. Of course, it was the National Foundation Weekend celebration parade and there were floats depicting the glorious history of Japan across the centuries. "Look," called Inu, "there is a Shinto float. Let's ask where we can find the shrines at Ise." "Well spotted, Inu, that will save us a lot of time!" said Yoko, slapping Inu on the back. The man dressed in traditional robes, walking at the side of the float, was approached and asked the question, to which he replied, "Are you the Hitachi Fuji-walkers who are coming to see me? Follow this float and we will be right there in time for tea this afternoon and we can talk then."

It was fun being part of the carnival procession. The country roads were lined with people waving and clapping. Yoko studied the Shinto float closely, as they cycled alongside. Surely this was the kind of thing they would need to build as a shrine, he thought. Meanwhile, the Kami, seeing Yoko studying the float and, perhaps, reading his thoughts, came over and walked alongside Yoko saying, "Young man, I think that you are getting some ideas of what the shrine to your father should look like, aren't you?" Startled by this seeming magic, Yoko blurted out, "Yes, Kami, but there are many questions forming in my mind."

"That is good, we will have a long discussion with you and your friends when we get to Ise in about one hour."

The Fuji-walkers cycled alongside the Shinto float, admiring the two huge, grey shire horses that were pulling it. The people lining the streets waved and cheered as the procession moved past. The young people felt like royalty, feeling that everyone was welcoming them!

Time flew past, the road was flat and even and, in no time at all, the shires were turning through a gateway into the broad drive of a homestead. "Welcome to Ise," said the Kami, as he turned to speak to two *petite* ladies who had come running from the house on hearing them arrive. "Park your cycles over by the stable where you can wash your hands and we will all have tea together." Kami called, as Egochi walked up to ask him where they could put up their tents. The Kami indicated a long sweeping lawn at the back of the house and Egochi joined the others in the barn, where much water was being splashed about in high spirits! "Come on, let's get the tents and our kit off the bikes. The Kami has shown me where we can camp," cried Egochi authoritatively. Soon there was intense activity on the back lawn, until Aisha, seeing the two *petite* ladies struggling to erect trestle tables said, "For goodness sake, can't you boys see that help is needed?" Inu, much to Yoko's annoyance, let go of the guy-rope that was holding up a pole at one end of the boys' tent and nipped down to see if he could help the ladies. Soon there was a large pot of green tea, surrounded by delicate porcelain cups and saucers, together with trays of cakes, bread and a variety of preserves set out. The Kami, now in a flowing black, silk robe, with gold dragons embroidered on it, came from the house and called all the children to come and help themselves.

Having eaten well and feeling satisfied with themselves, at having at last arrived at Ise and at receiving such a wonderful welcome, the youngsters were now anxious to see the shrines. Perhaps sensing the mood, the Kami, after a short conversation with the two petite ladies, walked across to the group of children and asked, "When you have had sufficient to eat, shall we inspect the shrines of Ise?" Immediately the Kami was surrounded by the group who followed his lead on to the long lawn which stretched down to a river. "Here is the ancient shrine of Ise," said the Kami, pulling aside a large woollen shroud, suspended over a rough-hewn beam of dark, red wood that joined two triangles of the same wood at their apex. "Shinto is literally the way of the gods and is the worship of natural things," explained the Kami, "and so, we have the natural cherry tree wood used and a shroud of wool from our own sheep. Inside there are no man-made idols, just a simple cherrywood table with a woollen coverlet and all set by the river, so that we may wash away all impurities." Rising, the Kami led the party out into the brilliant sunshine again, and, crossing a bridge over the river, he indicated the second shrine at Ise.

Egochi, himself feeling the effect of their long day, the good food, and the excitement at reaching their goal, approached the Kami and said, "Some of our younger members are feeling tired now, after the excitement of today, Kami. I wonder if you would forgive us if we turned into our tents for the night?"

"Of course, why don't you all jump into the river first, to experience the Shintoism of washing away your fatigue before you retire," replied the Kami. And so, Egochi, assuming what he considered to be his natural role, stripped off his shirt and led them all to the river, with a whoop and a cry of "Let's all get cleaned up and ready for bed!" Aisha stepped in, as she saw Egochi take Meija's hand!

The shire horses were calling for their breakfast as dawn broke over Ise.

Waking early to this pleasant sound, everyone was up, rested, and with a great deal of satisfied feeling, knowing that they had achieved what they had set out to do. And today they were going home!

Inu was the first to venture out, returning after a quick visit to the river to announce, "The two petite ladies have laid out a feast for breakfast for us and have said that we should all come quickly while the tea is hot!" On this news the boys were straight up, racing down the lawn to the river. Aisha gathered the girls around her, suggesting that they should help their hostesses after a wash under the outside tap.

The Kami smiled broadly as he arrived to see all the youngsters eating a hearty breakfast. He had changed into a flowing, green and gold robe with a matching headpiece, his long, tapering black moustache gave him the look of an Emperor. The children were awestruck in his presence. "Good morning, children, I have been thinking about you during the night," the Kami started. "In our Japanese culture we have a procedure called Ringi Nemewashi, which is a decision-making process passed down to us through generations of making Japan great," the Kami said seriously, "You have some important decisions to make in the near future. Perhaps I should explain Ringi means circulating documents and Nemewashi means touching all bases. Ringi Nemewashi is a means whereby management decisions are arrived at by circulating written proposals prepared by everyone. As proposals circulate, persons affix their seal indicating their agreement; this way everyone has an input to the plan and agrees to its implementation. Now, when you have completed your journey home, I suggest that you have a Ringi and Nemewashi to bring your project to a satisfactory conclusion," the Kami concluded. Yoko felt it was his place to speak up on behalf of them all. "Kami, we thank you for your advice and hospitality. We have all listened and learned and now look forward to inviting you to come to bless our shrine to Yamamoto-San on Fujiyama." "Goodbye and may the gods bless you all, I will look forward to your invitation," said the Kami, pleased with his weekend's work. Meija called the girls to assist the two petite ladies who were clearing away what little remained of the breakfast fare. Tents were taken down, folded and packed on their cycles with the rest of their kit. There were tears in everyone's eyes, as they bade fond farewells to their hosts at the shrines at Ise.

The road to Tsukiji was straight and flat, with no potholes or hills to slow down the jubilant youngsters. "Lets have a race," yelled Akao, a muscular twelve year old brother to Niku. Eight excited youngsters pedalled with all their might on, this, the last leg of their historic, fact-finding journey. "Phew! that is enough in this heat," said Inu after 250 metres for the sun was already high in a clear, blue spring sky.

Niku called out in support, "There is no hurry as we do not want to arrive at the old book-keeper's house for lunch all hot and dirty, do we?" And so, the pace slackened until the unmistakable perfume of the Great Tokyo Fish Market heralded their arrival in Tsukiji. "Where was it that the little, old book-keeper said he lived?" "First, let's find the sign for the "Association of Sushi Suppliers", and, then, his house is diagonally opposite, I remember," said Egochi, with a smug look at Meija.

Soon Egochi led the party to the house and found a group of young people already assembled in the front yard. "Are you the Hitachi Fuji-walkers?" enquired a young man, walking toward them with hand outstretched, "I am Hiroki Kato, leader of the Tsukiji Fuji-walkers, and my father said that you would be coming for lunch today. Come in, we have a lot to ask you."

Soon the two groups were joined in animated chatter with the Hitachi youngsters proudly showing their knowledge of Shinto shrines, their good friend, the Kami at Ise, while the Tsukiji group listened enraptured at the stories of their adventures.

The crashing of a gong from behind the house signalled that lunch was ready. Recognising Hiroki's father, the old fish market book-keeper, Yoko strode up to him saying "Hello again, Kato San, we have met your son Hiroki and told him of our very successful visit to the shrines at Ise."

There was much activity under the cherry trees as a line of tables was put up, covered and laden with yet another feast of Kaeseki Rori, the traditional multi-course meal of fish and vegetables.

"Look at this bed of glowing charcoal with delicious horse mackerel over it," called Egochi, whose digestive juices were calling for supplies! None of the youngsters needed calling to their meal, the Hitachi group still being questioned about their trip by the Tsukiji youngsters between mouthfuls.

What a party! Kato San moved among the young people, smiling here, nodding there and obviously enjoying the event. After two hours, noting that some of the Hitachi girls had seated themselves in the shade of the cherry trees, Kato-San called for quiet, as he had an announcement to make.

"I hope that you have enjoyed your meal. It has been wonderful to hear your stories and we would like to help you in the hard task you have ahead of you, building the shrine to Yamamoto San. After you had cycled off last Friday, I told all of my colleagues in the market what you were doing and, of course, many of them remembered Claude and wanted to help. Here take this," he said, handing a box to Yoko. "We had a collection to buy materials for the shrine, so here is about five hundred yen toward your task."

Yoko and the Hitachi group were stunned by this good fortune and did not quite know how to respond.

Kato-San suggested to Yoko that he keep the gift in the leather satchel that he offered. "You will not want to carry any extra weight on your ride home," he said. Yoko slung the satchel around his shoulders and asked, "How can we ever repay your kindness? Will you convey our thanks to all of Dad's old friends and ask them to visit

Hitachi in the future? This takes a big worry from our minds and I cannot wait to tell my mother about everything," said Yoko, offering his hand to Kato-San as he mounted his cycle. The old man walked to the gate with them saying, "Yes, you had best be off, to get home before nightfall, and I must get to bed to be up early and into the market by half past five in the morning."

There was a great cheer from their hosts, as the eight young cyclists set off. "We will meet at the shrine to Yamamoto-San when it is completed," they called to the departing travellers, before returning to clear away the remains of their feast.

The heat of the afternoon was tempered by the downhill slope as they freewheeled at the start of the final stage of their epic journey. "Inu, you are good at writing and spelling, will you chronicle this entire expedition?" asked Yoko, adding, "You could try to get it published in the newspaper as part of your training to be a journalist." Egochi cycled alongside Meija and the two spent the entire journey in deep conversation, as there was obviously a strong bond between them after their weekend together. "Mind you do not come off your bike again, Meija," Aisha called, keeping a watchful eye on those two. She knew that Egochi would soon be old enough to be called for military service and could visualise him, tall, proud and muscular in his uniform!

As they pedalled through the outskirts of Tokyo, Egochi pointed to a sign that read "To the beach". By general approval bikes were turned in the direction indicated and Meija said excitedly, looking over her shoulder at Aisha, "We could have a refreshing swim in the Pacific Ocean and still be home before nightfall." The hot, tired youngsters needed no urging and were soon on the beach discarding outer clothing and whooping into the ocean. The girls splashed the boys, who responded by ducking the girls' heads under water. The eight youngsters felt a common bond had grown between them all. They were good friends and, thought Aisha, "I will see that is as far as it goes!" "Time to leave," cried Yoko, to everyone's regret, as they pushed their cycles through the soft, yellow sand toward the road for Hitachi.

A cool breeze off the ocean helped the party on their way. At a stop to rearrange luggage on their cycles, it was decided that they would have some refreshment at the next roadside café. "We haven't eaten since lunch," Inu whinged. To which the girls responded in chorus, “Yes, but what a huge lunch we had with Kato San!” However, within an hour, they saw a sign for ice cream. “Now that is an idea,” Aisha agreed, pulling into a rather scruffy-looking garden, where there were men lounging on the front porch. The men were obviously drinking saki, so Egochi led the way into the house to order eight ice creams. Yoko followed, opening the satchel containing the cash from Tsukiji. “I am sure that my father would approve of us having an ice cream out of this,” Yoko said in a whisper to Egochi. “We have earned it, but keep your eyes open for that lot out there on the porch,” Egochi responded.

Returning to their friends with eight ice creams held high, the boys found that one of the drinkers was talking loudly to the girls, while Inu tried to stop him pulling Hoki’s hair ribbons. Egochi stepped between them, offering the ice creams to his friends. Four other drinkers staggered off the porch to see what all the noise was about. “You kids seem to have lots of money, bikes loaded with kit, washed and clean faces and able to afford twenty yen ice creams each,” said a short, dirty, little man with an evil leer “I expect you all have rich parents working in Tokyo and would like to share some of your good fortune with us poor working men?” he continued, adding, “give us your money. Let me see what is in that satchel and in all that kit you have loaded on your bikes!” Hearing this, Yoko clutched the satchel to his chest and moved closer to Egochi. “Leave those kids alone or I will call the police,” yelled the shopkeeper who had also come out to see what all the shouting was about. But the short, dirty man had grabbed Yoko’s satchel and called to his colleagues, “Look at this fortune these kids are carrying around with them. I expect they have been stealing all over Tokyo.” Yoko and Egochi tackled him to the ground and a fight ensued, the girls screaming and kicking at the men, as they pulled them off the boys.

Sirens wailed in the distance, stopping as two police cars skidded to a halt outside the shop and three policemen wielding their short, black night-sticks waded into the affray. Yoko and Egochi were the last to stand up, Yoko hugging his precious satchel with the Tsukiji gift in it. “You had best bring that to the police station to explain,” said the sergeant taking Yoko by the arm into one of the cars. “The rest of you stay here with your bikes.”

Egochi took control, asking the shopkeeper if they could come inside to wash and bathe their scratches and cuts. He then saw that their cycles and kit were in order and stacked them on the porch where they would be safe.

In a short while the cleaned-up youngsters emerged from the shop to find Egochi pumping up everyone's tyres. He preened, as Meija squeezed the back of his neck in a sign of affection and said, "You are so good to us all, Egochi, I do not know how we would have managed without you." "Let's be on our way," called Yoko, climbing out of the police car and pushing his cycle back onto the road for Hitachi. The cool of evening allowed them to make good time and very soon they were passing their school.

Arriving back in Hitachi was something of an anti-climax after their adventures! A few stray dogs sniffed around the village square but there was not a soul in sight. Six young lads ran into the square, playing "war". Seeing their older brothers and sisters leaning on their bikes, they ran off to their respective homes yelling, "They're back! they're back!".

This brought anxious parents into the square, where they bombarded their offspring with questions. Excited chatter ensued, until Inu's mother, a sad, slim, thirty year old lady, called for quiet. "I estimated that our young folk would be back at about this time," she said when all was quiet. "I have prepared a meal for us all. Come into my house, I expect our adventurers are starving hungry, and, by the look of them, in need of a wash."

Hoki and Inu led the way into their garden and pointed out the tap where they could all wash their hands. Meanwhile, their mother, assisted by all the parents, assembled tables and brought dishes of tasty delicacies from the house. "We have been treated royally wherever we have been," said Yoko, during a lull in the eating and drinking. Turning to Nana-San he showed her the box full of money in the satchel. "Look at all of this money, that was given to us by dad's friends at the Great Tokyo Fish Market, to use for buying the materials to build his shrine." "Yes, and they have promised to come to visit us when we have it finished, Nana," added Aisha. Hoki and Inu were deep in conversation and, putting down their plates, walked over to their mother. "Where is Dad?" Hoki asked and their mother encircled them both in her arms, replying, "Your father has gone to join the Imperial Japanese Army. He left on a big troopship the day after you went to Ise."

It was a proud but sad Inu that told the other lads this news and soon it was time for them all to return home to their own beds. Cries of "goodnight, goodbye, and see you at school in the morning" brought the evening to a close.

The school bell broke up excited groups of children's chatter as they filed into the main hall for assembly. The headmaster and staff looked down from the platform and sternly called for quiet before saying, "Yoko and Aisha Yamamoto, come to the platform." The two felt their hearts pounding as they did as they were told. The Headmaster then explained to the entire school exactly what the "eight brave adventurers" had been doing over the holiday weekend and asked for a report. Yoko, who had not expected this, grasped his sister's hand and mumbled that Inu had kept a diary and would be writing the full story for the *Hitachi Herald*. The headmaster seemed pleased and satisfied with this, sitting down, congratulating them all, adding that he was looking forward to reading the story.

School was quite a bore that Monday, of course, but they decided that they would hold a Ringi and Nemewashi, as soon as they got home after school. "Bring some paper and pencils *and ideas*," Egochi called out to them all as he put his arm round her waist and walked Meija home from school. The village square was quite empty, save for a few stray dogs, that evening, when they gathered for what Yoko called "our first business meeting". He had done quite a lot of preparation and, as he was Claude's son, decided that he would take the lead before Egochi did. "Remember what the Kami told us about the Ringi and Nemewashi being a process of making management decisions? Well, we have had a lot of fun and now must get down to making those decisions. First we must decide who is going to be the secretary, in charge of building our shrine, drawing the plans and ordering materials, as well as looking after the money we had from Tsukiji." Inu jumped up saying, "I will look after all the secretarial jobs, as that will give me information to make my story complete." They all nodded in agreement with this and Yoko suggested that they all write down the jobs that needed to be done and their suggestion for the person to do them. "Bring these to a meeting at the site of the shrine, overlooking Segura Bay on Fujiyama, on Saturday morning at ten o'clock. "Now we are getting somewhere," Egochi whispered to Meija as they dispersed.

*

The blue waters of Segura Bay sparkled in the bright sunshine of Saturday morning, when the youngsters gathered around Yoko's drawing of the shrine to his father which they planned to build. "I drew this up to show to Komatsu-San, whose factory makes earth-moving machinery and who was the president of the Fuji-walkers when my father was killed. He has offered to help us get the materials up Fuji and to dig any holes that we need." This news brought cries of wonder from them all! "Well done, Yoko, that will save my muscles," Egochi shouted. Inu had some good news too. "I have spoken to the editor of the *Hitachi Herald* and he wants me to write our story." Together they decided that Aisha should be the treasurer, responsible for paying the bills, when she told them that the headmaster had offered to keep the money in the school safe after their experience at the ice cream shop.

News of the war with the Americans was good! "Italy has joined in to help the Germans in Europe," Egochi stated knowledgeably, at a meeting of the Fuji-walkers. The work on building the shrine was progressing smoothly, thanks to Komatsu San, his workers and machinery. "Let us aim to have the official opening on December seventh, the first anniversary of my father's death," Yoko announced, as they climbed toward the site, and this was agreed.

Nana-San was pleased to hear this news, as her sister in Hiroshima had been sick and she planned to visit her there. Now she could do that and be back for the official opening and dedication of the shrine to her beloved Claude. Everything was working out well and she was very proud of her only grandson Yoko. Inu had the first instalment of his report on their journey to Ise printed by the *Hitachi Herald*, who had promised to send a photographer to the opening. Inu took his responsibilities seriously and had written to all of those good people, who had given them food and shelter on their journey, inviting them to come to the Yamamoto shrine in December. He also asked if the Kami would perform the dedication ceremony on that occasion. Komatsu-San offered to supply a traditional Kaeseki Rori meal for everyone, set up in large, white marquees, that could then be used by the visitors for overnight accommodation. This was a relief to the Hitachi Fuji-walkers who, having received such hospitality and good fortune, were anxious to repay their visitors. Inu was proud to show the replies to his letters to his comrades, as he really was not suited to the hard, physical work involved in the actual building of the shrine. Egochi, on the other hand, loved to strip off his shirt and flex his muscles in front of the girls, who were busy making the woollen shrouds for the shrine. A month before the date for the opening, Egochi announced that he had been called to join the Imperial Japanese Army. Meija was sad about this but very proud and the two youngsters were always together arm in arm walking on Mount Fuji.

It snowed on the morning of December seventh. Hitachi was alive with the Komatsu workers setting up marquees for the banquet. The Tsukiji Fuji-walkers arrived early, followed, soon after, by the group from the pretty homestead where they had first received hospitality. There was a great roar when the two huge, grey shire horses arrived in the square, with the Kami and the two *petite* ladies in the cart they pulled. Aisha and Yoko escorted these special guests to their own home, where Nana-San and their mother were pleased to fuss over them.

The opening was scheduled for noon and everyone was told of this, the blessing, the Kaeseki Rori and sleeping arrangements. "How sad that Egochi has to miss this day, Meiji," Aisha said, slipping a comforting arm through her friend's, as they climbed Mount Fuji for the ceremony. "Yes, but he is serving our beloved emperor, which Claude would have approved," she replied, with a sob in her throat. "The shrine to Yamamoto-San is magnificent and a credit to the young people whom he trained and to the people of Hitachi," the Kami said at the start of his address to the more than one hundred smiling people in the congregation. He continued to talk on the virtues of Trust, Loyalty and Honour, all of which had made Japan great in the past and, with young people like the Hitachi Fuji-walkers, the future of Japan was assured.

Komatsu-San had been invited to speak, out of courtesy and gratitude for his generosity, and he too praised Yoko, Aisha and the team, adding that there were jobs for them all with his company when the time came to rebuild Japan's future prosperity after the war!

These praises were still ringing in their ears when the children assembled at school to hear the same again from the headmaster! "I was pleased to hear what Komatsu-San had to say about employment prospects," he said.

Life in Hitachi soon returned to normal. Nana-San Yamamoto left for Hiroshima where she cared for her sister. Meija spent an increasing amount of time with Aisha and Yoko, who had been encouraging Inu with his writing, found that Inu's sister, Hoki, was now grown into a very attractive young lady! The two brothers and sisters formed the main structure of the Fuji-walkers now that Egochi had gone and younger children wanted to join the group, who had a focal point on the mountain with the shrine. Returning from the mountain one spring Sunday, Meija, Hoki and Aisha were troubled and Aisha led them into her house while Yoko kept Inu and the young lads in the square. Approaching her mother, Aisha asked her to come to the verandah to talk to the girls. "Meija is going to have a baby, Mama!" she said in a whisper for this is what she had always feared with Egochi courting her friend. Mother responded as mothers around the world respond when faced with this situation. She expressed the necessary degree of delight and advised that Aisha went with Meija to see her mother, who would make the best arrangements for the future. Meija was relieved to have been able to share her secret, and at the helpful response as the girls walked off.

There was a setback in the development of the war! the powerful Americans were pushing the Imperial Japanese Army out of the Pacific Islands they had liberated, and, every day at school, the headmaster announced that a pupil's father had made the greatest sacrifice that any Japanese man could make "to die for Japan". Meija worried and, just as they were planning to celebrate the first anniversary of the opening of their shrine, the news came that Egochi too had made that sacrifice. The Fuji-walkers rallied around and they particularly prayed for Egochi's soul when they next visited their shrine. In November, 1943, baby Egochi was safely delivered to Meija and filled the void in her life, as well as having so many "uncles" and "aunts" to spoil him. Sadness descended again when Inu announced that his father too had made the sacrifice. "But, at least, we have a new male member of the family."

Inu's story of building the shrine to Yamamoto-San was printed over the next six months in the *Hitachi Herald* and, having now left school, he was offered a job as a "cub" reporter, with the responsibility to write on everything that happened over a wide area around Hitachi. With his first month's wages, he bought himself a second-hand bicycle to help him cover the territory. "After all, my old one took me to Ise and back," he explained, apologising for such a seeming extravagance. Yoko revelled in continuing his father's work with the Fuji-walkers, bringing the young ones up to standard with camping and walking the mountain safely. Aisha loved baby Egochi and was a constant companion to Meija.

Nana-San announced that she would have to go back to her sister in Hiroshima, as she was now in hospital and there were her children to care for. "I do not know how long I will have to stay, but I must be there for her." Yoko was not too upset by this news as it meant that there was one less pair of prying eyes to avoid when he invited Hoki to his house for dinner. His mother liked Hoki and, having warned Yoko to learn the lesson of Egochi and Meija, was glad to see him growing in stature and confidence like his late father. They planned to have a happy first birthday party for baby Egochi, in spite of the fact that his father could not be there. And so it was that the baby had a happy childhood planned ahead for him. "We will make him the youngest ever Fuji-walker, Inu," Yoko announced at the party, "because you and I do not have our fathers either."

Inu's story of the Hitachi Fuji-walker's endeavour to build a shrine to their heroic leader, Claude Yamamoto, had been picked up by the Tokyo newspapers as an example to all Japanese children in these dark days of war. In consequence, Hitachi was receiving many visitors at weekends, in particular, all of whom needed directions to the shrine. Yoko organised his group as guides on the mountain, while Aisha and Meija with baby Egochi served refreshments at the shrine. This served two purposes, first as a source of a small income for Meija, as well as occupying the long summer months with her beloved baby.

Inu found that he did not have time for the Fuji-walkers now that he was out searching constantly for stories to write for the *Herald*. Yoko took the train to the Komatsu factory, where he was training to be a draughtsman three days a week. Komatsu-San had been so impressed with Yoko's courage, strength, and determination, after the loss of his father, that he had assumed a paternal role.

Nana-San was still in Hiroshima. Her sister had died and she had continued to care for the family, such was the strength of Japanese family feeling. Aisha and her mother missed Nana-San but understood her absence.

Inu brought news of the war to the village, for he was now able to obtain and read the National newspapers. Meeting Yoko at weekends he would pass the latest information on. Singapore had been captured, and Rangoon, in Burma, too! There was nothing that could stop a Japanese victory now. The two young men's fantasies were far removed from the days when they shaped their fingers into guns and shot enemy soldiers from the trees, as they ran home together from school. One weekend Inu had a particularly exciting piece of news for Yoko. He had discovered that a hero of the battles in Burma was a Major General Yamamoto. "It must run in the blood of your family," Inu said. Yoko, wondering what future heroism and success lay ahead for him, simply shrugged his shoulders.

The four girls, Aisha, Meija, Hoki and Niku, worked hard at catering for the visitors to the shrine, to where they pushed baby Egochi in his stock-laden perambulator every Sunday. "Soon we will have enough money to be able to buy a proper wheeled trolley to bring our needs," Meija suggested, as they sat looking down into Segura Bay one afternoon. "Yes, let us aim to get that by baby Egochi's second birthday next November, shall we?" Hoki joined in, all the girls looked on the baby as their own and a firm bond was forged between them.

The very first occasion they used their new trolley, Segura Bay was full of warships and sailors were coming ashore on leave. Hoki agreed to ask Inu what was going on and what it was all about.

The question was soon answered when a stream of sailors in uniform arrived at the shrine. There were some friendly, if cheeky, advances toward the girls, who had fits of giggles as they served the sailors with tea. An older sailor came behind the counter and asked who this Claude Yamamoto was. "He was my father and died a hero's death at Pearl Harbour," Aisha replied. The petty officer who had asked the question responded. "Our Admiral of the fleet is Isoroko Yamamoto and I will tell him about your father, so expect a visit from him when we have won this war." Aisha could not wait to tell Yoko, who then arranged to be at the shrine next weekend when the petty officer said that he would bring his mess back. "We have not seen such pretty girls for years," he added. Hearing this, Yoko decided that he would definitely be there! "Yes, we have had some fierce battles in the Coral Sea last year with the American Fleet, under their Admiral Chester Nimitz. We lost some of ours but sunk some of their ships, but that is war," the petty officer continued, "and we have just had a good scrap around Guadalcanal too." Yoko was fascinated to learn about Admiral Yamamoto's war exploits.

The Kami from the shrines at Ise visited Hitachi for the second anniversary of the opening of the shrine and it was decided that they would use the occasion to have him bless baby Egochi into the Shinto faith. "Now you are a real Fuji-walker Egochi," Inu said to the baby, as he and Yoko taught the child to walk down the mountain after the ceremony.

Yoko was proud to relay the stories of Admiral Yamamoto's battles to anyone who would listen! Inu was getting bad news stories from the war in Europe where the Germans, having swept into Russia, had been thwarted at a place called Stalingrad in the cold of a Russian February. It was a source of great interest to Yoko to learn details of the war's progress. Not all of it was good, though, but, fortunately, there were no Japanese soldiers fighting in North Africa, from where the Germans were being driven!

Many young boys and girls had joined the Fuji-walkers, and this kept the older members busy, training them in the history and folklore of Mount Fujiyama, first aid, climbing and patriotism. When the weather permitted, they would take their tents up to the shrine and camp for the weekend.

Planes roared overhead that weekend and the senior Fuji-walkers had difficulty in calming the young ones! There was an uneasy feeling in Japan, as news had got out that long range American airplanes had been bombing Tokyo and some of the main ports. Yoko sat all members down and reassured them quietly that all would be well, thinking to himself, 'This is what my father would have done.'

Inu was waiting for them when they returned from camp. He had some bad news from Europe! "The Germans and Italians have surrendered and the war in Europe is over!" he confided to Yoko out of earshot of the others.

Komatsu-San called Yoko into his office and explained that there was much work for his company to do producing heavy machinery to handle the work of repairing bomb damage. He suggested that the time had come for Yoko to leave home and stay in a company house in Tokyo.

It was a serious Yoko who returned to Hitachi the next weekend to discuss this with his mother. "I will be all right here with Aisha, and it will be good for your future to do as Komatsu-San suggests." Yoko was pleased with this, but what about Hoki? The two had grown very fond of each other over the three years since their epic cycle ride to Ise. She greeted his news philosophically, "Perhaps I will be able to get a job with the company, when we could get married and both live in the company house." Yoko liked this plan! Particularly when Hoki, Aisha and Meija suggested that they would take over the running of the Fuji-walkers!

A summer camp was planned for August, and Yoko promised that he would be home for that. "After all, I need a holiday too!" he said, as he left for Tokyo.

Life was not the same in Hitachi. Hoki, Aisha and her mother missed Yoko terribly, vying with each other for his attention when he came home once a month. Yoko was pleased to learn of their plans for summer Camp, high on Fujiyama for the first two weeks of August. "I will book my holiday for then as soon as I get back to the company." Yoko had qualified as a draughtsman, worked hard and had brought innovative ideas direct to Komatsu-San who was proud that he had recognised early the talent in the lad.

All bicycles and Meija's stock trolley were lined up for loading in the square at Hitachi to transport the group's camping requirements to the site. Yoko and Inu were proud of the way the girls had taken over and organised everything and they had prepared some contributions to the programme themselves. "It will be our main job to get the young ones bedded down at night, after the excitement of the events of the day," Inu offered, as he parted two boys fighting.

There was a great roaring that woke everyone up that night! A huge cloud of dust and smoke was in the sky to the south. "It looks like a big mushroom," Hoki cried, as she snuggled up to Yoko. "And that is what we will tell the youngsters it is until we get them home to their parents," Yoko responded, cuddling his love to him. Inu felt there was a story here and excused himself, promising to return as soon as he had news. Speculation had it that Fuji, the dormant volcano had erupted, but, when Inu returned four days later, he told them that it was a new super-bomb that the Americans had dropped on Hiroshima. Aisha and Yoko worried about Nana-San who was living in Hiroshima and it was a very uneasy group of young adults that tried to get the young ones to sleep that night. And then it happened again! It was agreed that they would end the camp and get back home to Hitachi!

It was an apprehensive Yoko who returned from his holiday. The second super-bomb had annihilated Nagasaki and Japan had surrendered! Komatsu-San called everyone together at the factory and explained that there was much for them to do to restore Japan to its former glory. "And it is up to everyone to work hard to achieve this," he said seriously, adding, "and there will be a great need for the machinery that we produce too!"

Yoko thought of his father and vowed that he would work to regain the pride that Claude had always taught his Fuji-walkers.

Five years went by and, under the guidance of Komatsu-San and the other major manufacturers, it worked! Life in Tokyo was good. Yoko bought a house for his mother and planned to marry Hoki, who also had a job with Komatsu.

The young Yamamotos prospered with Komatsu, Yoko became head of the draughting office and a respected member of the development board of the company. They decided to start a family "as the gods decide" and so it transpired that, after the birth of their second daughter, Komatsu-San called Yoko into his office. "I have been delighted with your work in developing our company, Yoko. You have always been full of innovative ideas and now I have a plan, to open a plant in Europe, that I want you to consider!" Yoko's mouth dropped, as a thousand questions raced through his brain. "I must give this a lot of thought, may I come back to you with some questions, after I have talked to Hoki and the children?" Komatsu-San offered a glass of Saki, nodding his head saying, "I knew and hoped that the son of my old friend Claude would answer like that."

Hoki was aghast! Sitting on a garden swing hammock, while the children played in the pool, they discussed the ramifications of moving to Europe for the company. Yoko had his clipboard and made notes of all the questions he needed to ask, so that they could arrive at a decision. In Hitachi, his mother was quite content and visited her grandchildren often. "You have been talking about placing a plaque to your grandmother in the garden of remembrance in Hiroshima," Hoki said, adding, "Perhaps we should do that before we leave for Europe, Yoko?"

That made up Yoko's mind! Hoki was for it. He would take his clipboard in to see Komatsu-San on Wednesday!

Komatsu-San invited Yoko to sit opposite him in his office. "You will have a lot of questions for me, Yoko, but first, I have one for you." Yoko was rather startled at this opening gambit because he had planned how he wanted the interview to develop. However, he dipped his head slightly and Komatsu-San continued. "Firstly, what did your young wife have to say as, now that you are a family man, Yoko, they must take preference." Yoko beamed when he explained that Hoki was as excited as he about the prospects, adding, "I have a list of questions to ask first of course." Komatsu-San dipped his head in understanding and invited Yoko to "ask away". The two men discussed Where? When? and How? at which Komatsu-San stood up and addressed Yoko's questions.

"We have grown prosperous here supplying the heavy building machinery to rebuild the cities of Japan that were damaged in the war, Yoko, and it was when you remarked that 'there must be a lot of opportunities for the company in Europe too' that I contacted our embassies throughout Europe, to make enquiries of the import/export potential for our products. Nothing much came of that for six months but, then, we heard from our ambassador in Great Britain that their Welsh Development Agency had big plans to bring employment to their Valley people, whose work in the coal mines had finished. They offered us big incentives to open up a factory assembly plant in a place called Taffs Well, near their capital city, Cardiff. They also have plans to build a whole new town on top of one of their mountainsides, which is where we would have a company house for you and your family. The ambassador spoke to me on the telephone, saying that "Newtown" was part of a green, green valley called Rhondda."

Yoko, with most of his questions answered, sat upright when Komatsu-San mentioned the salary and expenses package! "Hoki and I will have to start learning English straightaway," he blurted out, on hearing that English was the dominant language. The two men shook hands firmly, looking each other steadily in the eye, sealing the bond of trust that had started at the opening of the shrine to Claude Yamamoto on Fujiyama, ten years earlier. "Hurry straight home to your wife and have a good long talk with her before saying any more, as the ladies sometimes see things that we overlook in business," Komatsu-San urged Yoko, with a shrug of his shoulders. Yoko, heart pounding, needed no urging! His family sat in the garden and his oldest daughter, now past her first birthday, toddled excitedly over to him. "We are so happy here, Hoki. But wait till I tell you what the boss has offered us to set up an assembly plant factory in South Wales, where we will have a company house in Newtown, Rhondda Valley, which is beautifully green and we will share the prosperity of the company too, Hoki!" Catching Yoko's excitement, Hoki said she would bring some drinks for them all and walked into the house.

Long, cool glasses of orange juice were enjoyed quietly under their cherry trees full of blossom. Hoki sighed, "They had war over there too, we must remember, Yoko, and I just wonder:

"IS MY VALLEY STILL GREEN?"

"Let's get started on those English lessons."

Chapter Five

Newtown Rhondda

"Homes fit for heroes" was the cry, after the horrors of the First World War. But it did not happen! At the end of World War Two, the politicians decided that there had been enough suffering and an ambitious programme of building thousands of homes for returning servicemen and their families replacing bombed out cities was planned, in the shape of whole new towns with an infrastructure of schools, roads and hospitals, embarked upon. Welwyn Garden City in rural Hertfordshire, a pre-war experiment was used as a model, upon which the Bedfordshire Town of Milton Keynes, the Sussex Town of Crawley, and the Glamorgan Town, "Newtown Rhondda" were styled.

"I like this one, love," Marjorie smiled at Sid, as the estate agent showed them into number twenty-five, Hann Close, a four bedroomed house with a large garden, at the end of a cul-de-sac. "So do I," responded Sid, with a squeeze of his sweetheart's hand, knowing that the Farm Holiday Cottage business was in the good hands of their now forty year old son David and his wife Frances, who had ensured the continuation of the family name by producing two sons! Having spotted an interesting piece of property, in the shape of a redundant pub on the outskirts of Newtown, Sid was anxious to look into the viability of his new business idea! "I love the way they have curtained their windows opposite," Marjorie beamed, pointing to a similar house to the one they were in. "The one with the big Mercedes in the drive you mean?" Sid responded, his mind elsewhere. An offer was made to the agent for number twenty-five, with a request for a speedy response. "Our furniture is in store in Weston-super-Mare and we would like to move in quickly," was Sid's parting shot to the departing estate agent.

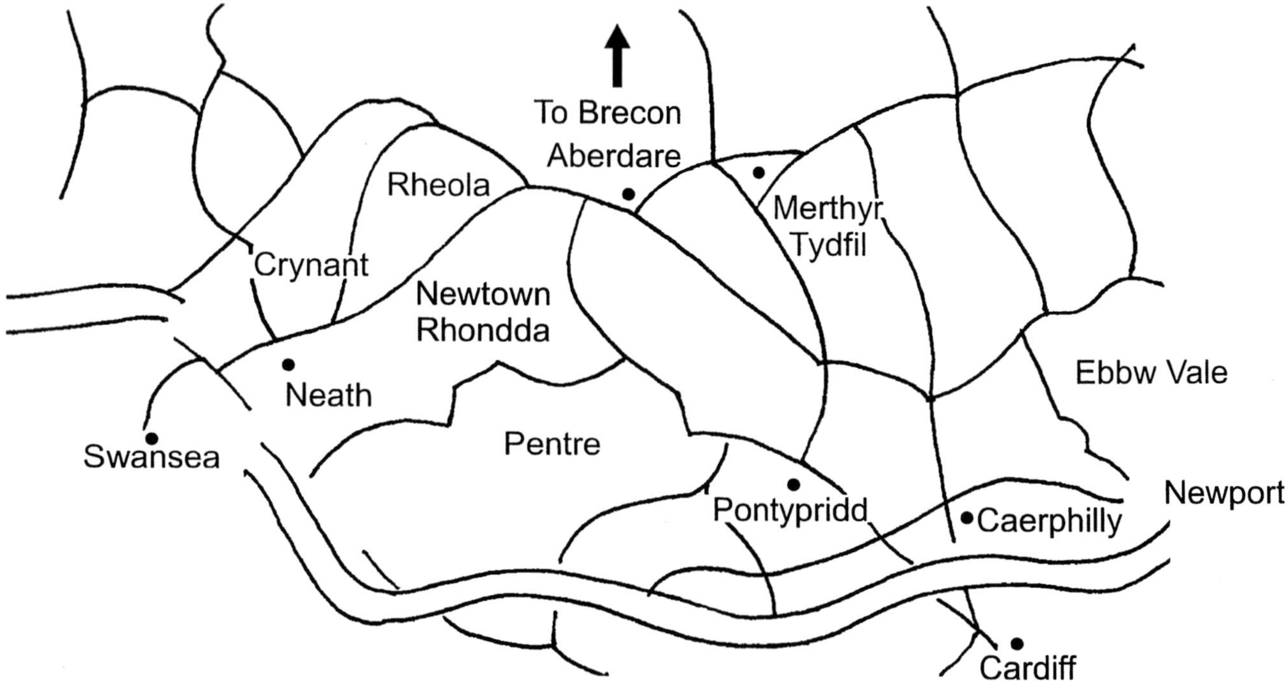
To Brecon
Aberdare
Rheola
Merthyr
Tydfil
Crynant
Newtown
Rhondda
Ebbw Vale
Neath
Swansea
Pentre
Pontypridd
Newport
Caerphilly
Cardiff

NOT TO SCALE

The report of the Monopolies and Mergers Commission into the licensed trade in the nineties had brought about a drastic change in the structure of the public house business in the United Kingdom. Many pubs had closed down and were boarded up, others had seen a change in their management structure as well as massive refurbishments, bringing in an era of traditional pubs with superb restaurants. Sid, always with an eye to business, wondered if they bought a redundant pub with a good car park, could they get planning permission to put two prefabricated units each of ten hotel/motel rooms in the grounds? He thought he had spotted the very place on the road that connected the Rhondda Vach (small) over the mountain top through Newtown and down to the Rhondda Fawr (big) at Pentre. Floating the idea to Marjorie, he gained the response, "For heaven's sake, we are now in our sixties. Can't we forget about new businesses and just retire gracefully?" Seeing the logic of this, Sid agreed, thinking, "I wonder where the 1st. Newtown Scout Group meets?"

The move from Weston-super-Mare was stress free; the removal men worked hard, placing our furniture where directed. Then Marjorie listed all the jobs that needed doing in the garden and a visit to a rather large garden centre we had spotted nearby was planned!

"Dai" Williams was the manager. A seventy year old, with a row of medal ribbons on his jacket, he could not have been more helpful. Enquiring where we were living, he straightened up noticeably, when we told him we had just moved into number twenty-five Hann Close, saying, "That will be opposite my boss, Hans Ludmeyer, and his family, who are in number twenty-three." Then he explained that "although he is a Jerry, he is a great fellow who I met in the war." We completed our purchases and Dai insisted that he would bring them round in the van "to save dirtying your car".

"This is what I have been waiting for," Guido beamed at his wife Eugenia, as she brought a bottle of Chianti, in an ice bucket, with two glasses, to the side of the swimming pool in their garden at number twenty-four Hann Close, Newtown Rhondda. "And you have earned it too," she responded, first checking that the children were quite safe as they splashed each other! For, in the past five years, the Managing Director of Bracchi's Company Limited had more than doubled the turnover of their company. Firstly, by gaining distribution and sales of Sidoli's Italian Ice Cream throughout all of Wales, with the support of four factories and a fleet of refrigerated lorries and, then, by the introduction of pizza to all of their by now thirteen restaurants. "What kind of Italian restaurant is it that does not sell pizzas?" he had demanded of his partners.

Now, having been asked to chair the South Wales Hotels and Restaurants Association and with the children, Ben, ten, and Vittoria, eleven years of age, the Pontypridd apartment was too small for their needs and they had moved into this nice four bedroomed house on the hill where there was a pool and space to entertain business colleagues and parents visiting from Italy.

"The chap next door, in number twenty-five said that he would ask the old guy, Dai, who helps in their garden if he would do a couple of hours a week for us, so that will be useful, now that you have agreed to go with Ben to run the Cub Scouts where he is the Group Scout Leader. He said his name was Sid, I think, English with a Welsh wife, seem a nice couple."

Gretta and Hans Ludmeyer were up early as usual this Monday morning. Hans, unable to keep away from his demanding job of the reafforestation of South Wales, snatched breakfast with their family, Otto now thirty-nine and Rose, thirty-eight, before pulling his company Mercedes out of the drive.

"I saw the estate agent showing some people around number twenty-six yesterday, Hans, and I think they were Chinese, they had two daughters about the same age as Otto and Rose." Gretta called out to her husband as he left, first for the Garden Centre they had set up, with Taffy Williams to manage for them. He would then continue on to his office at the Welsh Development Agency and not be home until late evening. "Did you say that Chinese people were looking at number twenty-six Gretta?" Hans questioned, as they sat for their evening meal. "Guido will not be too happy if they are planning to set up a restaurant will he?" They had made the acquaintance of their neighbours, Guido and Eugenia Sidoli, when they held their Ruby Wedding dinner in their Pontypridd restaurant. What an evening that had been! Angharad Williams was obviously nervous as she accompanied Taffy to the party. Gretta, putting her at ease, had noted her newly coiffured hair and best dress. Gerda and Marlene refrained from speaking in German. As he paid the bill after a superb meal, the cashier asked Hans if they lived in Hann Close, Newtown. It transpired that they were neighbours, at which Eugenia was called and a fresh bottle of wine shared, with Taffy admitting that he was "going to do some gardening for the Italians". "But only because they buy their stock from the Garden Centre, Hans," Taffy whispered to his friend and employer!

"A night to remember" was the verdict of them all at coffee, back at number twenty-three, with Marlene, Gerda and Angharad in a fit of giggles as Gretta checked with Myfanwy, who had now moved in as cook/housekeeper, that all was well. Eugenia and Guido took up the invitation to call in for a "nightcap", when they got back to the Close and Hans, Taffy and Guido enjoyed each other's company in "man talk". "I have been admiring your Mercedes Hans," Guido stated over a glass of "Niersteiner", German wine, "supplied by the company I work for," Hans replied modestly, going on to explain what his job was in Wales. "I can tell you some stories about Hans, whom I first saw down the sight of my rifle many years ago!" Dai "Taffy" Williams broke in, giving his boss a slap on the back. Hans laughed, turning to Guido quite seriously, "Gretta told me that the agent was showing some Chinese into number twenty-six this week, Guido, and we wondered if we were going to have a Chinese restaurant in Newtown?" Guido, who kept his ears and eyes very close to the business scene in the Valleys replied, "They are Japanese, in fact, and he is the Development Director of the new plant in Taffs Well for "Komatsu", the earth-moving equipment manufacturers. "I met him at a civic reception, name of Yoko Yamamoto, about our age, Hans." Eugenia and Gretta arrived, interrupting this "man talk", knowing that it would inevitably lead to "business talk". "Taffy, you are neglecting Angharad who I think is ready for bed," Gretta spoke to Taffy crossly which had the desired effect and everyone said "goodnight", wishing the two ladies a safe journey home tomorrow."

It was two more weeks before several lorries bearing the name "Komatsu" arrived at number twenty-six. Curtains were hung, furniture moved in, followed at the weekend by Yoko and Hoki Yamamoto with their two daughters.

Sid found that Scouting in Newtown was no different to anywhere else! Shortage of money necessitated the constant need for fund raising. A shortage of adults prepared to give up leisure time to become leaders, had seen his offer to "help with the group" readily taken up and a warrant as Group Scout Leader issued! Pleased with his success at recruiting the Italian lady, Eugenia Sidoli, newly moved into number twenty-four, as a helper with the Cub Scout Pack. When

Marjorie mentioned that number twenty-six was now occupied, he took an early opportunity to introduce himself to the occupants. "Yoko and Hoki Yamamoto from Japan. He is a director at the new Taffs Well Komatsu plant and they have two little doll-like daughters, probably about twenty-five years of age, but it is difficult to tell with Orientals!" Sid reported back. "And, oh yes, he did a lot of fell walking as a lad and could be a useful one with the Scout Troop!" Marjorie smiled saying, "Give them time to get their clothes hung in the wardrobes first!"

"Scouts plan pig roast at their August fête" was a headline in the free *Newtown Rhondda News* where the group had taken a quarter page advertisement. When Sid talked to Guido over the garden fence, and they had a beer, Guido had offered to do this, as Bracchi's contribution to the group for the right to run the refreshment tent. Scouts in uniform were organised to distribute advertising leaflets and posters, which Yoko had kindly supplied from his company. "Well, he did offer to help!" was Sid's response to an implied criticism.

Hans reported back to Gretta on his progress with his job and some of the work he had put in. Covering scars left on mountainsides by the removal of coal tips was an outward sign of achievement because, as he explained to Gretta, "trees take decades to grow and this work is for the benefit of our grandchildren really". That said, he recalled the pattern of footpaths that his father had marked out before the war, and how the Hitlerjugend had enjoyed using them. "I am going to work out a series of forest walks that will show the beauty of my work as I take local people to where they can see rivers, waterfalls and reservoirs in my green valleys," Hans announced to Gretta, as they sat after their meal one warm summer evening. "Yes, and perhaps some clearings with picnic tables?" Gretta encouraged her husband. "I could do the same for the motoring public too, by advertising and signposting scenic drives to picnic areas with car parking," Hans enthused. "Don't forget some toilets too, Hans!" the ever practical Gretta interjected. Hans had encouraged his wife to take up the nursing sister's job she had been offered at the new cottage hospital and they discussed at length their problems and aspirations in their respective jobs. With Myfanwy moved in, the Ludmeyers loved their new lifestyle. Hans had been approached by the relatively new "Green" political party and had a fellow feeling with them and their policies of preservation and conservation. He had agreed to stand as their Councillor for Newtown ward of the Rhondda Borough Council at the local elections next May.

Yoko went to the Scouts with Sid, finding the Welsh lads very much like his Hitachi Fuji-walkers. He agreed to become an Assistant Scout Leader with special responsibility for hiking and mountaineering activities. The two leaders would pop into the Owen for a beer after a hectic Friday Troop night with their thirty-six Scouts. They saw Dai Williams, and got into conversation with the man he was with, whom they both felt they recognised from number twenty-three. It was, of course, Hans, who became most interested in their uniforms, explaining that Adolf Hitler had banned the Boy Scouts, when he came to power, and asked what they did. Learning, with amazement, of Yoko's experience in fell walking and his special responsibility with the 1st Newtown Troop, Hans outlined briefly his scheme to establish forest walks. The four men agreed to meet in Sid's house on Sunday, bringing their wives, to exchange ideas and make some plans. "After all, it is for the kids, isn't it?" Yoko concluded.

Marjorie and Sid ushered everyone into the conservatory overlooking the garden as they arrived, and coffee was served. Guido and Eugenia were the last to arrive with their girls. Sid suggested, "Can I take this opportunity, now that the Hann Close committee has met, to ask your help with the pig roast and fête on August 14th?" There were amused glances passed between neighbours, whose offspring were playing badminton happily in the garden. Hans was the first to speak. "Amazingly enough, Sid, August 14th is my sixtieth birthday, and I can think of no better way for us Welshmen to spend the day, perhaps with a swift half in the Owen in the evening?" "Thanks, Hans, funnily enough, I will be sixty on August 11th," Sid responded, turning to Guido who had already agreed to run the pig roast and refreshment tent anyway. "Snap" was the quick answer from Guido, who declared that he too had just passed his sixtieth anniversary! "Time for us to leave these old gentlemen and advise the younger generation on the finer points of badminton," Marjorie winked at the ladies, taking up a carton of Cokes and walking into the garden.

"Isn't it wonderful how well our children get on together?" Gretta remarked, as Marjorie matched up the two Japanese girls and Vittoria against Otto and Ben for a "round robin knockout match". Hoki laughed saying how much she and Yoko were loving their new life now that they had such good friends and neighbours, adding, "We were a bit lonely at first but now we are part of Sid's Hann Close Committee, it is heaven!" Eugenia asked Marjorie if she would mind "if everyone came over to number twenty-four for a barbecued "brunch", when all the youngsters could have a swim". This agreed, the men were advised and Hans and Taffy nipped over to number twenty-three to "get a bottle or two of fine German wine!"

Enjoying the freedom of their neighbour's swimming pool, Aisha and Meisa Yamamoto whispered to each other, while standing in the shallow end watching Otto Ludmeyer preparing to dive his muscular body off the board at the other end. Their attention had not gone unnoticed and Otto swam quickly toward the two girls, engaging Meisa in animated conversation, asking if he could bring some soft drinks for them both to sip in the shade of the late July sunshine. Meisa nodded her approval, whilst keeping an eye open for the arrival of her mother! Aisha, helpful to her sister, wandered over to little Vittoria to practice their English, while her brother, Ben, helped put the plates of salad out ready for their visitors to arrive. Hans and Sid were deep in conversation as they arrived. Hans had some exciting news. The parks and gardens section of the Welsh Development Agency, where he worked as head of "Forest Enterprise Wales", learned that their bid to stage the National Gardens Festival in Ebbw Vale had been accepted and all senior officers of the W.D.A. and their wives were to be presented to her Majesty the Queen, when she came for the opening next Spring! "What an honour, Hans," Sid said in congratulations, as Hans had spoken about his work when he had taken on the Chairman's job at the first Newtown Scout Group, explaining that his twenty year contract was coming to an end and he would now have time for other things in the community. Guido called out to his friends to pour some drinks for them all while he was cooking the steaks! "Bit of a busman's holiday for you, isn't this, Guido?" Sid responded, taking his friend a glass of Chianti. Eugenia gave a sly grin as Guido did not cook at all these days, the businesses being under firm management.

The ladies were buzzing around Gretta asking about her visit to see the Queen! "What will you wear?" Marjorie asked, suggesting that the four of them should go on a shopping trip to Cardiff in good time beforehand. A puzzled frown came across Hoki's face, as she noticed her daughter laughing and chatting with Otto. "We must keep an eye on those two, Gretta," Hoki suggested to her neighbour who assured her "they will be okay".

The afternoon passed very pleasantly and Sid, fearing the purpose of the meeting was escaping them, brought up the matter of the August fourteenth fête "not forgetting that jar in the Owen that we promised Hans" he concluded, as volunteers were gained for all of the necessary jobs on the day. Chairman Hans concluded Scout business saying, "I think we should make up to £500 if the weather holds."

In the event, it rained! The refreshment tent and the Pig Roast took a lot of money and Guido made a £500 donation to the Group insisting that "if it didn't rain would my Valley still be green?"

There was a mass exodus of the younger generation of Hann Close in September! Otto had gained a place at the University of Wales, Cardiff, to study Forestry. Aisha and Meisa Yamamoto, having decided they wanted to teach, also went to Cardiff where they had secured places at a Teacher Training College, sharing a flat. Hoki, mindful of her friend, Meija's experience in Hitachi, talked very seriously to her daughters, comforted by there being "safety in numbers". To which Yoko had responded, "That did not stop Egochi!" Ben Sidoli left for Italy to work with his grandparents in Rabiotti's restaurant, which, with Guido's money, initiative and drive had developed into a holiday complex with accommodation, concert theatre, swimming pool, as well as several themed restaurants to cater for all ages. "I want you to go out there, learn the business, see if your grandparents are coping as well as they insist they are, and give me a full report on what else we could be doing in the Amelia area" was the briefing Guido gave to his twelve year old son, confident that he was "a chip off the old block."

Gretta enjoyed the attention she got having been seen on television in the company of the Queen of England and talked excitedly about it to her mother on the telephone! Hans was busy canvassing for May's election, standing as the Green party's candidate for the Rhondda Borough Council (Newtown Ward).

Improvements had been effected at the headquarters of First Newtown Scout Group, which was quickly becoming a community centre in the absence of such a provision for the town. A new kitchen, meeting the Common Market imposed standards, had been installed. A playgroup met there every weekday morning, sequence dancing for senior citizens took place two afternoons a week, and

Marjorie had started a badminton club, the floor having been painted out as a court. Thus, life in Newtown Rhondda was meaningful and busy!

Guido Sidoli had become restless! The businesses were making good profits, Sidoli ice cream now had national distribution and he was fending off the big competitors wanting to take him over. Eugenia had joined the badminton club and the Restaurants Association resisted his plans "to drag it into the twenty-first century". Even his little Vittoria had joined the Scouts, following that Association's decision to allow girl members! Guido tried golf, joining the Llantrisant Golf Club, and finding great comradeship there but feeling he needed a new challenge, invited his accountant, Jack Howells, to "join him for a round of golf and a chat about the future of Bracchi's Company Limited".

Jack Howells painted a glowing picture of the state of the company, adding, "but I understand your restlessness, Guido, coming from a family who walked from Italy to Wales with nothing but hope as a goal!" The two men talked at length over a drink in the clubhouse. Jack, shaking Guido's hand, left, saying, "I have an idea forming in my mind, based on the current 'back to basics' feeling of nostalgia that is around. Give me a week and I will come up with something."

"Do you remember your grandfather's first order in the first Bracchis they set up in 1933?" was Jack Howell's opening question to Guido. "A rock cake and a cup of tea for tuppence," was the instant response. Noting Guido's puzzled frown, Jack continued to explain that the business was founded on inexpensive, wholesome but basic food, well served adding that this was what people still required in the new recession of the last quarter of the twentieth century. "Not that I am suggesting that you specialise in rock cakes, Guido! Rather that you put yours and your partners' energies into producing a simple, basic but enticing menu, much as you have at present, and then offer franchises in Bracchi restaurants in every town in South Wales. Since the mines closed, there are a lot of hardworking Welshmen with their redundancy money to invest in their futures and, with the Bracchi name so well established already, I am sure there would be plenty of takers. You understand about franchises, I know, and I think you should hand the project over to your partner, Carlo Fulgioni, once your board has agreed in principle."

"We could even lend them the money to buy the franchises from us, Jack!" was Guido's reaction for he was a true entrepreneur, recognising that money is but a commodity that should be used! Carlo welcomed the challenge, now married with three children himself, he knew that he still had unused talent to spare.

The *South Wales Echo* headline screamed "Green Valley man awarded the O.B.E. in the New Year Honours" above a photograph of Hans Ludmeyer, with the story of his achievements in his chosen profession. Yoko was the first to cross the road to congratulate Hans and escort him to the Owen for a pint. Guido, Sid and Taffy had been telephoned to be there too and much hilarity and friendship ensued! Joe, the barman, brought a tray of drinks over to them, "Congratulations, Mr Ludmeyer, have these on me," he said with a wink to Taffy. The five men stood to take their drinks, Taffy introducing Joe with "this is my grandson whom I have never told you about." He continued to explain that Myfanwy had had a baby by an American soldier in 1943 and they had kept this secret for all this time, such was the shame of sex before marriage at that time! Congratulations were given to Taffy now and the conversation switched to how things had changed in the Valleys, indeed, in the world, since the end of the Second World War.

"It has been over for fifty years in June this year" was the realisation and they all decided that there was much to celebrate, setting about making plans for a grand celebration in Newtown. Hans, exhilarated with the news of his award, which he recognised would help him in the election, apologised that he was too busy "talking on doorsteps and stuffing envelopes" to do very much to help, adding, "but when I am on the council, I will have a lot to put into our community." Guido suggested that they organise a party at Scout Headquarters. "We could hire a funfair for the morning, serve a cooked lunch for the Senior Citizens, have an "Its a Knockout" competition in the afternoon, followed by a slap up tea for the children, then a grand dance with a Glen Miller style band in the evening." This excited them all until they considered the cost of such a celebration! Guido spoke up "Look, friends, I have just franchised the business that my grandfather started before the war, when he told us "how green was my Valley". Now that I have turned that green into gold, let my company pay for this to prove "my Valley is still green".

Handshakes were offered all round at this, warmly and firmly taken and received by the five elderly men.

Only Yoko appeared to hang back, noticed by Taffy, who quickly interjected "Of course, your war did not end until August did it, Yoko?" Hans, appreciating the chill at this realisation of the horror of the atomic bombing of Hiroshima, added, "All of us had our lives dramatically changed by that awful war when we were all enemies, but now we are all friends, successful, happy and fulfilled, lucky to discover the answer to our question."

"IS MY VALLEY STILL GREEN?"

"I will drink to that," said Taffy, the only native-born Welshman among them, raising his glass.